My Life Without Perfection

Joy G. Love

Editors Margaret Kennedy and Laura Dial

PublishAmerica
Baltimore

First printing

ISBN: 1-4137-6050-3
PUBLISHED BY PUBLISHAMERICA, LLLP
www.publishamerica.com
Baltimore

Printed in the United States of America

In memory of
Dr. Reed O. Dingman, MD.
1906~1985

Acknowledgments

Without the skills and work of Dr. Reed O. Dingman, I would have never lived through the adventures of plastic surgery.

I deeply appreciate my parents' love, understanding and patience during my years of development.

When I began to research the area of plastic surgery, I visited the medical library at Vanderbilt University in Nashville, Tennessee. It was there, within the medical library, I met Mary Tehol. Mary Tehol and her staff assisted in locating materials concerning the history of plastic surgery and orthopedics.

Dr. Victor L. Yu, MD is a professor of medicine at the University of Pittsburgh and chief of infectious disease at the VA Medical Center in Pittsburgh, Pennsylvania. Dr. Yu offered me articles that he had written concerning Serratia marcescens.

Crystal Smith at the National Library of Medicine in Bethesda, Maryland, made phone calls and gave me assistance in locating materials. I am grateful for her time and effort.

Mary M. Hartman is a reference librarian at the Maurice and

Laura Falk Library of the Health Sciences at University of Pittsburgh. She was very helpful in the location of the United States Government articles concerning the research conducted with germ warfare.

Ms. Kay Hogan Smith is an associate professor/librarian at the University of Alabama at Birmingham. She assisted in the location of articles on Serratia marcescens.

Mrs. Recia W. Taylor at Quillen College of Medicine Library in Johnson City, Tennessee, assisted in location of materials to review while writing this book.

My friend Deborah Hurst, PhD helped in locating information. Dr. Hurst works for Griffin Hospital in Derby, Connecticut.

Dr. Paul L. Schnur, MD is a plastic and reconstructive surgeon in Scottsdale, Arizona, who was kind enough to allow me to use information from the web site on the history of plastic surgery.

Dr. Robert Oneal, a plastic surgeon at St. Joseph Mercy Hospital in Ann Arbor, Michigan, was helpful in locating articles written by Dr. Dingman.

Dr. Louis Argenta was very helpful in releasing my plastic surgery chart. Dr. Argenta is chief of plastic surgery at Wake Forest University in Winston-Salem, North Carolina. If I had a question on a procedure, Dr. Argenta would come through with the answer.

Allen Underwood, a local businessman, was wonderful in giving me computer guidance.

Ann Boyd Stewart, major gift officer, Department of Surgery University of Michigan was helpful with quick information in answering last-minute questions.

In locating the pictures, Douglas Sexton and Sister Ann, who work in the audio visual department at St. Joseph Mercy

Hospital in Ann Arbor, Michigan, were very helpful.

The Bentley Historical Library at the University of Michigan was helpful in the location of pictures of the University of Michigan Medical Center in the 1960s.

I appreciate the editing skills of Margaret Kennedy and Laura Dial.

I am grateful for the encouragement from Carey Barr and Dr. John Moore, a plastic surgeon in Franklin, Tennessee, who read the manuscript and offered advice, which was helpful.

It was a great and rewarding experience for me. I am grateful to all of my caregivers throughout my life, and words will never express my gratitude.

I am very honored that PublishAmerica accepted and published my manuscript. I appreciated their staff and their efficiency in answering all my questions during the publishing process.

Table of Contents

Introduction

The outbreak of World War II changed the world forever, leading the United States and the former Soviet Union to become superpowers. With the end of the Cold War and the fall of the Berlin Wall, the United States stands alone as a superpower.

My story begins during the height of the Cold War. At the end of World War II, the United States, England and Russia begin research on germ warfare.

I have researched the development of Serratia marcescens and it origins and how this germ was released onto the American public during the 1950s. The release of this germ is of vital importance to me; it shaped my future.

After I was born in 1958, I contracted Serratia marcescens. I have written this book about of the twenty surgeries I had to undergo in order to correct the damage caused from this so-called harmless germ, Serratia marcescens.

I will cover the plastic surgery and reconstruction of my face as a child during the 1960s–80s. These surgeries were very severe and very rare. I will cover the history of plastic surgery and other fields of medicine.

Throughout my life, I have had a major battle with dyslexia. I will explain the test used in my case and how I was able to achieve my college degrees with severe dyslexia. I will also give a review of my life and the struggles I had in obtaining employment.

I filed and won an EEOC case against the Department of Justice Bureau of Prisons. I wrote this book to help others who may have a disability or those who have a disabled child. I also hope that professionals who work with the disabled can benefit from this book.

I hope this book will reflect some light on the world of a person with a disability and show that in spite of the disabilities, accomplishments can be made.

Chapter 1
Cause of Problem: Serratia Marcesens

"Welcome to My World" was a song sung by Dean Martin, the entertainer and singer. Within that song a line was sung: "Miracles I guess still happen now and then." How true this is! Now I welcome you to my world—a miracle did happen.

As I sat quietly on my sun porch, I began to think back, to my childhood, my dreams, adventures, and my failures. I want you, the reader, to get an understanding and a glimpse of my life covering the surgeries performed. It would take too much time to cover every event concerning my life. I will touch only on the ones that have made a significant difference.

As a child and adult, my heroine was Helen Keller, for she opened many closed doors for the disabled and gave us all encouragement. There were others in my life who assisted and helped in my development: my parents Mansell and Betty Love, and Dr. Reed O. Dingman. Without the plastic surgery performed by Dr. Dingman, my life would have been much different.

I was born on February 24, 1958, in Ypsilanti, Michigan, at Beyer Memorial Hospital. I was two months premature, weighing only 4 pounds. I remained at Beyer Hospital for 5 weeks. I required intermittent oxygen therapy due to pneumonia.

I was home only 7 days before being admitted to the University of Michigan Hospital. I had begun to vomit after each feeding, to the point that it had become bile stained. I was taken to the emergency room at the University of Michigan Hospital and surgery was performed. They expected to find a blockage within my bowel, but this was not the case. The doctors discovered that I had an infarcted right paraovarian, or ovarian cyst, in the right lower quadrant with hemorrhage and adhesions involving the cecum and distal ileum. During this surgery a large cyst the size of an egg, was discovered on my right ovary. It had twisted over my intestines, cutting off blood supply to the area. The cyst was removed and the adhesions severed. Today my arms, head, and ankles still retain the scars from the tubes that were placed into my body. Doctors worked very hard to save my life and later to repair the damage caused from the infection.

During the several weeks following surgery, I continued to struggle with inflammation of the lungs and other complications. I was treated with blood and serum proteins. After several weeks of repeated blood cultures, they revealed Serratia marcescens.

Serratia marcescens had gotten into my blood stream and into my mandible (lower jaw). It had fused my temporal mandibular joint. I will be referring to the temporal mandibular joint as the TM joint. It took 4 years for Dr. Reed O. Dingman to develop the techniques to repair my jaw. I was 7 years old when Dr. Dingman did the surgery that released my TM joint;

this allowed me to open and close my mouth correctly. I would undergo another 5 major facial surgeries. I also had a deformity in the left hip that caused a shortening of my left leg. I wore an inch and half lift until age 34. I had two major hip surgeries and one right knee surgery. My sternum was scraped and I had a right ventricular type A shunt. I had, in all, 20 surgeries to correct the conditions Serratia marcescens caused.

The first known case of infection from Serratia marcescens occurred in 1950 when Mr. Edward Nevin, a 67-year-old who lived in the San Francisco Bay area presented with flu-like symptoms. He later died of Serratia marcescens. At that time, the Navy was shooting Serratia marcescens into the air, allowing the germs to travel over the population. A healthy person who came into contact with this germ would have symptoms similar to the flu. While a person who was ill or may have had recent surgery, as I did, this germ could enter into their blood stream. This germ becomes devastaing in the blood stream.

Serratia marcescens was also released into the New York City subway system by breaking a light bulb in which the germ was located. This was reported on *60 Minutes* in 1980.

Serratia marcescens can be a deadly biological germ. This germ can occur naturally in plants and other organisms. The following definition was given for Serratia marcescens:

A gram negative bacterium that is very common in soil and water; most strains produce a characteristic pigment, prodigiosin. Opportunistic human pathogens, infecting mainly hospital patients.[1]

Serratia marcescens is being recognized with increasing frequency as a cause of serious infection in man. This microorganism dates back to the time of antiquity. Because of its red pigment, it masqueraded as blood. Serratia marcescens is an aerobic, motile, gram-negative bacillus classified as a member of the division Klebsiella-Enterobacter-Serratia. They are capable of producing pigment, the intensity of which ranges from dark red to pale pink, depending on the age of the colonies.[2]

In 1950, Serratia marcescens was thought to be harmless but this would quickly change. In 1964, it was recorded on one hospital survey of Klebsiella-Enterobacter-Serratia infection. Only three infections were listed and Serratia marcescens was listed as the cause. In 1968, there were 15 cases of Serratia bacteremia recorded in the medical literature. While Dr. Victor L. Yu reported 76 cases of Serratia bactermia in one hospital alone from 1968 to 1977. Serratia marcescens will produce pigmented colonies that look like drops of blood on food stuffs, especially the starchy variety.[3]

A journey back into history shows that as early as the sixth century B.C., Pythagoras noted the appearance of blood coloration in foodstuffs. In 1800, Ehrenberg found 100 historical references to the miraculous appearance of blood on food.

Serratia marcescens was found in Eucharistic bread in 1169 in Denmark. This starchy sacrament was located within a damp environment of medieval churches and was an excellent area for the growth of Serratia marcescens. Eucharistic bread represents the body and blood of Christ. In 1264, a priest in Bolsena, Italy observed the red substance during mass as the Eucharistic bread dripped the red blood-like substance. This was written into a story by Raphael in his fresco *The Mass of Bolsena*.[4]

In 1819, this blood-like source appeared in an Italian peasant home. The entire household was frightened; crowds had gathered outside their humble little home. As any place then and now, rumors began to spread. A supernatural power had caused blood to spring from the polenta because it had been made from cornmeal that had been hoarded during the famine of 1817, and it was not handed out to the hungry people. Bartolemeo Bizio, a young pharmacist, demonstrated that the blood was caused by a living organism, which he mistakenly believed to be a fungus. Bizio named this organism Serratia marcescens, in honor of an Italian physicist Serafino Serrati. Marcescens is derived from the Latin word *to decay* since Bizio observed that the pigment deteriorated quickly, dissolving from a light-pink material into a purplish red, viscous form.[5]

During the years that the Cold War was growing, there was a build up of defense weapons including biological weapons. There were many universities doing biological weapons research. England and Russia were also involved in biological weapons research.

The United States Army, in order to study the effects of Serratia marcescens on the general public in 1950–1951, had United States Navy ships release Serratia marcescens into the ocean waves, and it was blown inland to San Francisco. Monitoring stations isolated the organism from as far as 80 meters inland. It caused hospitals in San Francisco to experience outbreaks of Serratia marcescens.

Doctor Richard Wheat, MD reported 11 cases of Serratia marcescens urinary-tract infections of patients at Stanford University Hospital in San Francisco.

In that same year, Serratia marcescens was used covertly in aerosolization experiments in Calhoun County, Alabama, and Key West, Florida. The numbers of reported cases of pneumonia reached a record peak within those counties.[6]

On April 30, 1980, I learned while watching a program by *60 Minutes* about the spread of Serratia marcescens. My case had not yet been connected to the spreading of the germ. There is the possibility that the Department of Defense was doing experiments within the area that allowed me to contract Serratia marcescens.

In doing research for this book, I learned that during the 1950s the Department of Defense spread Serratia marcescens widely across the United States. There were many different methods that were used to release this germ. Serratia marcescens with its ability to cling to clothing and to flow through the air could get into heating and cooling systems within homes, offices and other buildings.

From a German article, I learned that Serratia marcescens was of concern for newborns, especially those who were premature. "That Serratia marcescens until the 1950s was considered as a pathogen for humans. Since then the organism has been reported repeatedly as a cause of nosocomial infection." The article stated how Serratia marcescens was resistant to usual antibiotics, causing treatment to be difficult; the infants were premature and suffered severe infections of Serratia marcescens.[7]

I was born within the decade of all the experiments. World War II ended with the defeat of Germany, Japan, and Italy. It was feared in 1943 that Germany could be planning to use biological warfare.[8] This caused the biological warfare research to be moved at a much faster pace. The United States emerged from World War II as a superpower, and so did the former USSR.

As the United States entered into the Cold War era, no human experimentation had begun. Human experimentation was being planned and discussed. Two small-scale outdoor tests with two biological simulations had been conducted. One of those simulations was BG, a spore forming micro-organism, and the other was called Serratia marcescens, a vegetative organism commonly referred to as SM. These used inert material such as talc, and were conducted at Camp Detrick, Frederick, Maryland. These materials were considered to be totally harmless by the scientific and medical experts of the period.[9] When the Cold War began, the United States began to build up defenses in case of an attack, including the study and buildup of biological weapons.

In 1949, construction of an enclosed one million-liter test sphere (the largest in the world) was built at Camp Detrick, and biological warfare explosive munitions tests with pathogens were started.

In 1950, U.S. naval ships in the Atlantic Ocean off Norfolk, Virginia, released clouds of Serratia marcescens to envelop the ships. This was done to assess their vulnerability and to test prototype BW (biological warfare) electronic detection devices.

In May 1958, the JCS again reviewed the biological warfare and chemical warfare situation at the request of Defense Secretary Neil McElroy. During 1958, biological and chemical warfare programs were established to prepare and research the development, for the testing, and distribution of the Serratia marcescens.[10]

The following places and dates are of special interest to this author. There are many locations where these biological warfare chemicals were developed and tested.

1. Henry Ford Hospital, Detroit, Michigan
   July 1951
   Oct. 1952
   July 1952
   July 1953

2. Michigan State College
   May 1956
   Dec. 1965
   May 1960
   Sept. 1967
   Nov. 1968
   May 1961

3. University of Michigan
   July 1951
   June 1952
   April 1953
   Sept. 1955
   Aug. 1959
   June 1964
   Aug. 1962
   June 1964
   Nov. 1965
   March 1967
   July 1961
   June 1969[11]

During the biological testing, many of the shipments were made by the United States Post Office and the United States Public Health Service along with commercial airlines. However, there were more restrictions placed on military shipments as to their packing and handling. The earliest packaging regulations for etiologic agents of the U.S. Post Office in 1951 applied to "specimens of diseased tissues, blood, serum, and cultures of pathogenic micro-organisms." Military operating procedures for shipping biological materials were first known to have been published by Fort Detrick in

1950–1951, and by the Department of the Army in technical Bulletin 237 dated 6 June 1952. These source documents have not been provided to this author. It is important to note, however, that the earlier non-military regulations and standards primarily addressed packing design criteria rather than reliability factors. Accordingly, in 1954, Fort Detrick initiated a review of procedures and regulations issued specifically for transport of infectious materials in the biological warfare program. This was due to the report of leakage of experimental living poliomyelitis virus in a commercial shipment on 24 May 1956 (at Washington National Airport). The U.S. Public Health Services on 15 March 1957 issued a federal regulation specifying packaging standards for infectious micro-organisms exclusive of postal mail.[12]

I understand the buildup of biological warfare, but I don't understand why it was used on the American public. One reason, I am sure, was to see the effect of biological or chemical weapons if released during warfare in the United States. The scientists of that period thought that Serratia marcescens was not a threat to anyone, but if one would look at my case they would differ with that assumption.

There is growing interest concerning Serratia marcescens, and research is being conducted worldwide concerning the outbreaks of this pathogenic that can infect the bloodstream of humans:

> The spread of SM in the 1990's occurred in a small hospital located in Saint-Etienne France. Eight babies and four mothers were found to have SM. It was learned to prevent an outbreak that the delivery room should have the hygiene of surgery rooms.[13]

The following page contains a copy of the letter I received on April 30, 1980, from the CBS program *60 Minutes* concerning the testing of Serratia marcescens. Twenty-first century America faces more threats of biological warfare from new developments around the world. When Richard M. Nixon was elected President of the United States in 1969, he stopped all the biological warfare testing in the United States.

CBS/BROADCAST GROUP

CBS Inc., 51 West 52 Street
New York, New York 10019
(212) 975-3166

Marjorie Holyoak, Director
Audience Services

April 30, 1980

Dear Ms. Love:

I am replying to your letter regarding the 60 MINUTES segment "The Death of Edward Nevin."

Thank you for expressing your interest in this report on an experiment in biological warfare; it is gratifying to learn that our journalistic endeavors are appreciated. We regret that we have no information on whether germ warfare experiments were conducted in Detroit or the Ann Arbor area.

Although we cannot be of assistance, we hope that you will continue to find 60 MINUTES informative and engrossing.

Cordially,

M. Holyoak

Ms. Joy Love

CBS Broadcast Group CBS Television Network, CBS Entertainment, CBS Sports, CBS News, CBS Television Stations, CBS Radio

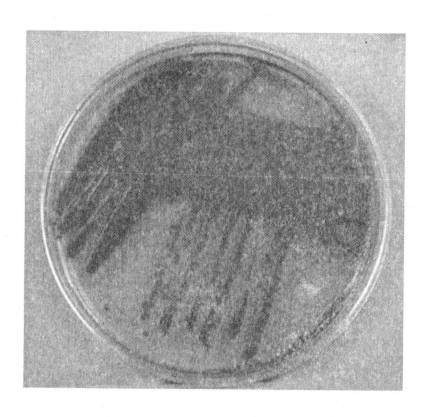

Picture of Serratia Marcescens courtesy of
Dr. Gary E. Kaiser, PhD, professor of microbiology.
The Community College of Baltimore County, Catonsville
Campus Baltimore, Maryland.

Beyer Hospital in Ypsilanti, Michigan, as it looked in 1958. Permission to reprint given by Ypsilanti Historical Society archivist Jerry Pety.

Chapter 2
Childhood 1960s and Adolescence 1970s

People often may reflect back upon their childhood and adolescence. Even though I had multiple disabilities, that wasn't the focus of my life. The disability only became an issue when time for surgery arose. My hidden disability, dyslexia, proved to be worse than the physical problems, for dyslexia could not be corrected with surgery.

Rearing a disabled child is like rearing any child except you have a few more difficult steps that have to be taken. The parent must make sure that the child placed into their care receives a balanced childhood with much encouragement and understanding without pity. As a child I was taught how to face a very diverse society, how to meet this challenge, and above all how to socially function.

I had one older brother who was eight years older than me. My brother and I are very close. During my childhood I enjoyed watching him play football, basketball and baseball. He was very good in athletics. Within my home there was a lot of love and understanding and above all much laughter.

I achieved learning many skills; one was riding a bike with a hip problem I learned how to shift my weight, and that allowed me to have balance while riding. The other was how to ice skate.

I had developed a friendship with the family next door, and during my childhood the Johnsons became very special. I had a second home, and the Johnson children loved to tease and play with me. They were older than I was and always made time for me.

I had my disagreements as a child, and my parents remained out of them. Which was good! There are some who feel that a child with a disability should be treated specially. That is not always true.

A child with a disability must learn that other people have feelings too. Just because a child has a disability, they should not always be given their way. I was fortunate to have had both my parents. My mother was a stay-at-home mom while my father was employed with General Motors. There was a misconception that the factory workers were all uneducated. The truth is there were many people with college degrees working within automobile plants because of the excellent pay and benefits. My father was not an uneducated man. He was also a veteran of World War II; he served in Europe during the war and was wounded and received a Purple Heart.

Growing up with a face disfigurement could be very painful at times because of remarks made by other children. I was always told you have to overlook those remarks. There were many times that was very hard to accomplish. Most of the children I grew up with accepted me.

All children look at themselves in a mirror, and boys do it just as much as girls. We live in a society that places much emphasis on one's appearance. I often would stand and try to imagine what I was going to look like. Many times I would pull my cheeks out sideways to see what effect that would have on my appearance. I must say that I was way off as to how I would finally look. I learned later how the surgery was going to be performed.

I was reared in a subdivision. There were many different cultures within Ann Arbor and Ypsilanti. Some came to work in the factories while others came to work and attend the surrounding universities. Eastern Michigan University was one of the top universities for special education. The University of Michigan was rated highly in medicine, as well law and engineering. I enjoyed meeting people from different cultures and learned from their culture.

I started school at Holmes Elementary School in 1963. I remained in Holmes until 1966, my third grade year. I was then placed into Roosevelt School from fall of 1966 through 1969, for my fourth and fifth grade years. The school was located on the campus of Easter Michigan University. PhDs and student teachers from Eastern University were my teachers. I returned to Holmes for my sixth grade year. I really missed the interaction with lots of older students, and I especially missed the instruction of the PhDs and student teachers.

I began my seventh grade year at Edmonson Junior High in Willow Run. I only remained there for one year. My family moved to the west side of Ypsilanti after living on the east side for 13 years. There I began my eighth grade year at West Junior High School in Ypsilanti. I graduated from Ypsilanti High School in 1976.

My friends and I played board games and cards; we all enjoyed playing ball or just hanging around. I would stay out from morning until almost dark playing during the summer.

Whenever I developed an interest in a hobby, I received encouragement from my parents. I loved keeping tropical fish, and I still keep tropical fish even to this day. I now keep saltwater fish. I collected rocks from different parts of the United States. My father and I planted gardens; it was there that I developed my interest in plants.

I also had gotten involved with book clubs and an explorer club, which sent interesting boxes with maps and information about different nations throughout the world.

I had two dogs as a child. I found my first dog, Sally, in a cardboard box. We had been playing in an open field. When we looked inside we found a small black cocker spaniel.

My second dog was Mutt. My friend Dale Johnson gave him to me. Mutt was a small black and white puppy that was so ugly he was cute. I named him Mutt and we became friends; Mutt became my advocate. I could tell him anything. Whenever I was mad at someone, I would tell Mutt all about it. Mutt would sit and turn his head and listen to every word.

Just before the second surgery on my face surgery in 1969 (I was 11 at the time), my family had taken a trip to upper Michigan. The Johnsons were caring for Mutt. A storm came and Mutt became scared and jumped the fence and was struck by a car. It was very hard for Mr. Johnson to tell me that Mutt was gone. I often remember running and playing with him and the many times I could go out and give him a big hug around his neck, which made the world all right.

I also had a pet parakeet from a breeder near my home. I named him Tweety; he would kiss you and ride on your shoulder. Tweety was an excellent talker and learned to say my name. He did have one bad habit. He liked to curse. I'm sure if my parents knew about his foul language abilities Tweety would not been a part of our family. Tweety lived a parakeet's entire life span of 16 years and was buried in the flower garden of our new home on the west side of Ypsilanti.

My family and I often went camping at White River, Canada, many times during the 1960s. It was there I enjoyed fishing and often observed fish coming from the depths of cold clear water to bite the hooks.

I experienced many changes within the United States during the 1960s. I observed the Vietnam War as it was televised across the nation and around the world. I experienced the 1960s protests at Eastern Michigan University and the University of Michigan. In order to get to Roosevelt School I had to walk onto the campus. Roosevelt School was located next to the dean's residence. One day we were locked in our school due to the protests. Students were released to their parents one at a time. I do not remember being scared. I was just curious as to what was going on around me. I'm sure my mother was frightened by the experience.

I watched the civil rights movement and riots within major cities on television. By the end of the 1960s I truly can say that I lived through a social change within the United States.

During my childhood the automobile factories were one of the main sources of income. I feel that the late 1950s and 1960s were the heyday for the automobile industry. This all began to change in the 1970s as jobs turned more to technology.

I sat and watched TV with great interest as Apollo 8 circled the moon. I, along with millions around the world, watched as Apollo 11 landed on the moon.

I went to the local A&P store and purchased a 45 record of speeches made by President Kennedy about going to the moon. I was so happy to get this small record home. There I could listen to President Kennedy and the astronauts speak as they landed and walked upon the surface of the moon. The darkness and vastness of the moon interested me. The moon to me was no longer a faraway place, and the great mystery was gone. I will always remember when the American Flag was placed on the surface of the moon and how it looked like a board because there was no air blowing to make it wave.

The 1970s were very different. We were living in a new house and new neighborhood. I had to make new friends and get adjusted to a new school.

In 1970, my older brother Gary had gone on a trip to Florida where he met his soon-to-be wife, Peggy Meersseman. Peggy was from St. Clair Shores, Michigan. They now have four daughters and enjoy their grandchildren.

During the summers of 1972–1973, when I was 14 and 15, I volunteered at the University of Michigan Mott's Children's Hospital. This was a rewarding experience for me and I received a 200-hour pin for my hours of service.

Adolescence is a hard time for anyone, and I was no different. I had my ups and downs. Because of my disabilities, my life was altered as to the activities I could or could not participate in. I learned to accept this. I am not going to say that it did not cause some pain in my life. You have to move on and accept life. Life is not always fair.

We traveled out west during the summer of 1970 and enjoyed visiting Yellowstone National Park, The Little Bighorn in Montana, along with Dead Wood, South Dakota, and Theodore Roosevelt National Park in North Dakota. I had become very interested in history and enjoyed visiting the many historical sites and museums in the west. I will always remember the 1960s and 1970s and the many kind-hearted people along the way.

In high school I had developed many friendships. I did not have a steady boy friend during high school. I was always focused on going to college, and many of my friends had the same plans.

I did have one young man who would visit our home. He enjoyed playing dominos with my father; I preferred watching television.

I belonged to different organizations that allowed me to meet many people from the different high schools within the area. There was an event in Grand Rapids, Michigan, where my parents were the chaperones. We had a station wagon load of 10 girls who were taken to the Pantlin Hotel. I am sure my parents were glad to return to a quiet house. Everyone loved to tease my father; most of my friends called him IGOR, though no one knows or remembers or will confess to where that name came from.

I remember having parties at my home. Having to clean the house before the event and after was not my favorite thing to do, but we always had a good time.

After high school I worked with theater groups doing stage props and painting. With my interest in art, I often attended the Ann Arbor Art Fair. The streets were closed off and I could walk for blocks enjoying viewing the art and talking to the artists.

I further developed my interest in painting but lost my interest in theater. I enjoyed watching performers at theaters and clubs with my friends, but I had no desire to paint any backdrops or build any more sets.

I started Washtenaw Community College in 1976–1977. I transferred to the University of Alabama from 1978–1979. I will always remember the University of Alabama. When I arrived it was in August, and the heat engulfed me as I walked about the campus. I had to get adjusted to the heat. My dorm did not have an air conditioner. It took a week to get used to the campus, and I had to walk everywhere because I did not have my car. My roommate was from North Alabama and was a nice person; we have lost contact over the years. One memory I have was going to a very special homecoming gathering and hearing Coach Bear Bryant of Alabama speak to the students, and also seeing famous professional football athletes and other alumni from the school. I can't remember the exact reason why that homecoming was so special. At the time I did not know who all the famous football players were.

When I began attending the University of Alabama, I became involved with Campus Crusade. This was through friends who had invited me to attend the events in Tuscaloosa. Some of the football players attended the same small church. We often talked about football at social events. They were all very nice young men. Many of the players were also involved with Campus Crusade. I traveled with this group to Daytona Beach on spring break and visited Disney World in Orlando. It has been years since I was a student at the University of Alabama, but few a years ago I returned to the campus and visited with a former history instructor.

In 1980 I left the University of Alabama because of a health problem that will be explained in later chapters. In 1980 I returned to Washtenaw Community College. I received an associate's degree then transferred to Eastern Michigan University and received a degree in history. During my last semester at Eastern Michigan University in 1982, my father was diagnosed with cancer; he died on October 4, 1986.

While attending Eastern Michigan University, I continued going to Campus Crusade. During this period I had become involved with the activities within my church. I became a member of the Native American Student Association. I often attended pow wows and Native Law American Day at the

University of Michigan. I was interested in the history of the western tribes. During these years I made friends who were full-blooded Native Americans. I often think about my Navajo, Mohawk, and Chippewa friends, who visited our home frequently. Our family always enjoyed their company.

I was accepted into the School of Natural Resources and Environment at the University of Michigan in Ann Arbor. I developed many friendships with the instructors, staff, and students. I have remained in contact with some of the students I met. My instructors worked through my problems with dyslexia and helped me to develop my skills. I worked very hard to achieve my goal, and I was expected to do so. During this period I worked two jobs, and I did not have very much free time.

My friends loved to tease me. One particular friend used to sit around and think up jokes to make whenever he would see me. He used to say that he came by to roast me. We would always have a good time making jokes back and forth. We would go out and to eat and just have a good time. I always had a good sense of humor and have always found people who loved to laugh and joke. Even today in Tennessee I have friends who come up with something funny to say. I would worry about them if they didn't. Life is too short to be sad, and we all need laughter once in awhile.

In 1976, I traveled to the Silver Dome and listen to a sermon given by Rev. Billy Graham. The Silver Dome was filled to the rim and it was a very special time for me.

I had the pleasure of attending many lectures given by special guest speakers who were famous entertainers and politicians who visited the University of Michigan and Eastern Michigan University.

In 1976, I enjoyed the 200th Celebration of America's

birthday. Because of my interest in history, I was overwhelmed with the many events being shown on television and taking place throughout the nation. I tried to collect as much material as I could in regards to the events going on around me.

I often attended history lectures and spent much time visiting museums concerning events of WWII. I spent time doing oral interviews of World War II veterans and enjoyed listening to their stories. I found the veterans to be some of the kindest people you could ever meet. I still enjoy listening to those tapes.

I feel that history is an important subject. I spent many hours listening to history books on tape. I feel that a nation that does not know its history is lost. To understand today, you must know and understand yesterday.

Joy, front yard on Hunter, 1965.

Joy washing the car, 1965.

Joy fishing at White Lake, 1965.

Yellowstone vacation, 1970.

Yellowstone vacation, 1970.

Joy and Mutt, 1969.

Joy and Tweety, 1965.

Last Home in Michigan.
On the west side of Ypsilanti.

Chapter 3
History of Plastic and
Reconstructive Surgery

Since time began people have looked at their reflection in pools of water or mirrors. Appearance was important, even to the ancient people. Historical evidence for more than 4000 years cites medical treatment for facial injuries. Physicians in ancient India were utilizing skin grafts for reconstructive work as early as 800 BC.[14] As time advanced, many different types of deformities or injuries helped in the development of plastic and reconstructive surgery.

The United States' first plastic surgeon was Dr. John Peter Mettauer, born in Virginia in 1787. The United States was a growing nation, but during this period most of the better medical doctors were located in Europe.

The United States was advancing in many different medical fields. One such step began in 1827, when Dr. John Peter Mettauer performed the first cleft palate operation in the United

States using the instruments he designed himself.[15]

I feel that Dr. John Orlando Roe stated it best in the nineteenth century by saying:

> ...how much valuable talent (had) been...buried from human eyes, lost to the world and society by reason of embarrassment...caused by the conscious or in some cases, unconscious influence of some physical infirmity or deformity or unsightly blemish.[16]

What is plastic surgery? It is not "artificial." It is not plastic. This term comes to us from the ancient Greeks who have given the world so much in art and culture. The term *plastikos* means to mold or give form. Plastic surgery includes two methods— reconstructive and aesthetic subspecialties.[17]

The beginning of the twentieth century was a profitable time for the United States. Many new and creative inventions from automobiles to electricity, new home appliances and advancements in hygiene and medicine were being rapidly developed.

The United States found itself facing a war in Europe. President Wilson asked Congress for a declaration of war to allow the United States to enter into World War I.

Much of America favored going into World War I. The Germans were becoming too aggressive and the pressure was felt in America. In 1917, America entered World War I with high hopes. The American Army marched off as bands played and flags were waved. The English and French welcomed the newly trained troops. Upon arrival in Europe, American troops received brief training from the Allies. The American troops were then introduced to the horrible reality of trench warfare. The development of new and more powerful weapons used during World War I caused many injuries to the head and face region. The field of plastic and reconstructive surgery began to advance rapidly.

Dr. Harold Delf Gillies was born in Dunedin, New Zealand, in 1882, and died September 10, 1960 in London, England. Dr. Gillies attended Cambridge University. Dr. Gillies' interest was in otorhinolaryngology (earn, nose and throat), but World War I quickly changed his interest to plastic surgery. Dr. Gillies traveled to Paris, France, to study with the leading European experts of that period. Dr. Gillies became a leader in the field and development of plastic surgery. When Dr. Gillies returned to England he began practicing plastic surgery while still in the British Army. By 1916 he was established as a specialist in plastic surgery at the Cambridge Hospital, Aldershot, England.[18]

In the twentieth century came the development of Thomas Edison's light bulb, allowing more light. This allowed the surgeon to see to perform surgery more efficiently. During this period, surgery was being performed with no antibiotics or blood transfusions.[19]

Dr. Jakob Lewin Joseph, second son of Rabbi Israel Joseph, was born in 1865 in Koningsberg, Prussia. Dr. Joseph died in 1934. He went by the name of Jacques Joseph, and began working in Berlin, Germany, as an assistant to Dr. Julius Wolff, an orthopedic surgeon and professor.

During the period he worked with Dr. Wolff, Dr. Joseph became interested in facial plastic surgery. A distressed mother came to him concerned about her son's very large ears. The young child suffered from remarks made by other children about his ears.

In 1896 Dr. Joseph reduced the child's ears and thus began a career in the field of plastic surgery. Two years later he reduced a young man's nose, which had caused him much anguish, so much he would refrain from going out in public. Dr. Jacques Joseph called a desire to look normal "anti-dysplasia," not vanity. People with facial deformities could certainly understand the desire to look normal. Dr. Joseph became known worldwide when he worked at the Charity Hospital in Berlin. After World War I, Dr. Joseph became known as the father of plastic surgery. Dr. Joseph stated the following: "that anti-dysplasia was a treatable disease" and that what most people with a disfigured face want is to look normal.[20]

Dr. Ferris N. Smith, an otolaryngologist who had worked with Dr. Gillies during World War I, returned to the University of Michigan where he wrote a paper titled "Plastic Surgery." He presented his paper in the 1920 meeting of the AMA section on laryngology, otology and rhinology.[21]

Dr. Reed O. Dingman was born November 4, 1906 in Rockwood, Michigan; he died on December 24, 1985. Dr. Dingman received a DDS degree and a master of science in oral surgery at the University of Michigan School of Dentistry, and a MD degree from the University of Michigan School of Medicine. Dr. Dingman completed his residency at the University of Michigan in oral surgery and was certified by the American Broad of Oral and Maxillofacial Surgery in 1940. Dr. Dingman's interest changed toward plastic surgery. He then took a surgical internship at Washington University, Barnes Hospital, under Dr. John W. Kemper and Dr. Ferris N. Smith. The American Board of Plastic Surgery certified Dr. Dingman in 1949.

In 1964, Dr. Dingman developed the section of plastic surgery in the Department of Surgery at the University of Michigan, where he served as chairmanship of the section for

12 years. Dr. Dingman was the head of plastic surgery at the University of Michigan Hospital and St. Joseph Mercy Hospital in Ann Arbor, Michigan.[22]

Dr. Dingman, the man, was kind and humble. His goal was to understand you, the patient. He wanted the patient to fully understand what was going to be done. He took time and listened to questions, concerns, and fears from the patient and the family members. With fatherly words he could place everyone's minds at ease. He was a man who was brilliant in his field. I was a small child at our first meeting. At that time I could have never known the effect this great surgeon would have on my life. Dr. Dingman was known and respected both nationally and internationally.

Chapter 4
Oral Surgery and TM Joint Released

By 1960s I was being seen in Oral Surgery at University of Michigan. Oral Surgery at that time did not have any ideas about what to do. My mother was informed that the best that Oral Surgery could do would be to place cartilage on my mandible to improve my appearance. There was never any hope concerning my temporomandibular joint (TMJ), which was fused together, and because of this I was unable to open and close my mouth correctly.

God moves in strange ways. The family dentist informed my mother that he would not be able to care for my teeth and directed her to make an appointment with an orthodontist.

After the orthodontist examined me he, said there wasn't anything he could do for me. My mother said, "If she were your child, what would you do?"

He replied, "If she was my child, I would take her to Dr. Dingman." Then he said, "If you would like I will make you an appointment with Dr. Dingman." The orthodontist was given permission to make the appointment. And from that period on, until the death of Dr. Dingman, I was his patient in plastic surgery.

Dr. Dingman was quick to explain to my mother that she should not allow anyone to perform surgery upon my face for they might operate on the wrong side and cause me more damage. Dr. Dingman was concerned about my dental care. My deciduous teeth were discolored from medication that I had been taking. I was sent back to Oral Surgery at the University of Michigan from that point on only for dental care, where it was decided to remove my deciduous teeth.

November 20, 1963, I was admitted into the University of Michigan Hospital in Ann Arbor, Michigan. The oral surgery to remove my deciduous teeth was done on November 21.

I always enjoyed playing around the pediatric wing, but after this operation I looked in the mirror and discovered that I no longer had teeth. I was totally devastated by that, so much so that I wouldn't go and play with the other children. I was under my hospital bed crying when my mother arrived to take me home. This was not like me.

She had a small Mickey Mouse recorder player. As I crawled out, she sat down and asked, "Why aren't you playing with the other children on the sun porch?"

I looked into her blue eyes with a much bluer heart and told her, "I have no teeth." Then she understood the problem. With a smile she began to talk to me.

I had been told they were only going to remove a few of my teeth I understood what that meant. I did not think they were going to take all of them and only leave me four teeth.

The oral surgeon came into the room and tried to console me. As we left, he wanted to make friends with me again. He tried but to no avail. I felt double-crossed. I returned home with instructions to gargle with saltwater; this would allow my gums to heal.

When we reached the elevator I was still upset. An older man was on the elevator. My mother explained that my father had no teeth and had to wear false teeth, and if I drank lots of milk my teeth would, in time, return. I began to feel sorry for my father and totally forgot about my problem. The older man on the elevator laughed as we all traveled to the next floor and headed out the door.

It was a beautiful November day that on the 22nd. As my mother and I were driving back home from the hospital down Geddes Road, a news bulletin came over the radio that President John F. Kennedy had been assassinated in Dallas, Texas. America came to a stop and mourned, as did the world. It was a very scary time for the United States and the world. The big question at that moment was what was going to happen next? It was a time that America prepared to face the unknown future.

My next visit, like all the other previous visits, would include a number of other appointments that day at the hospital. I went from bone and joint, to ophthalmology, and on to plastic surgery. They would begin at 8:30 in the morning. First I would go to ophthalmology to have my eyes checked because I had a lazy eye. Then I went off to orthopedics.

If you had other appointments you had better let the staff know. This allowed you time so you wouldn't be late for the next appointment. I remember looking about a large room for a seat. There were many people waiting to be seen.

A large open window with blinds allowed the sunlight to shine across the room. There were many books for children to look at and magazines for the adults. After you sat awhile you lost interest in the books and magazines. There was a large fan that stood in the corner that I watched as it turned back and forth. I looked out the window across the lawn to a small brown building where the plastic surgery was located. Nice bushes landscaped the lawn. A blue bus with University of Michigan written on its sides traveled up and down the service drive along with small vans to assist visitors in reaching the hospital from the parking lot.

A nurse escorted my mother and I to a very small examining room. A doctor entered, asking me to walk up and down the hall. Afterwards a measurement of my left leg was taken and a few questions asked. It was decided to place a small lift in the left shoe to allow me to become more level as I walked. This also was helpful for the alignment of my back. I had a spinal cord that was like a snake.

After I was finished in one department, I moved on to another appointment. When I was sent to X-ray I had to follow the yellow lines on the floor. To reach a certain department you had to follow a certain color line on the floor. The walk to X-ray seemed like a mile to me just following that yellow line. I learned my way around that hospital at a very young age.

After reaching X-ray, a line of people was sitting in hard plastic chairs along the wall. A person sitting behind a small window was given a paper and my hospital card. If I was lucky, I could be out of there before lunch. This waiting area was located in a long hallway. I could sit and observe medical staff and patients going about their day-to-day routine. Doctors would walk by talking with other doctors. I could hear orderlies talking with nurse aids as they pushed stretchers by. The wheels were always squeaking and the patients lying on their backs always seemed to be watching the lights pass by above them on the ceiling.

Some patients asked, "Where are we going?" Wheelchairs

would pass with IV bottles hanging from a pole located on the back of the wheel chair. The nurse's aide or orderly would tell the person, "We are almost there." I used to feel sorry for some of them; they would look so tired and ill. I learned that you could always look around and see someone in much worse shape than yourself.

A warm stir of air would travel down the hallway, and I could smell the food in the cafeteria. After sitting in those torture seats for several hours, even the smell of the hospital food made me hungry.

The plastic seats were horrible. They were even bolted to the floor. I wondered about that. No one was going to bother to take one of those torture seats.

Finally, I was called in, and in a few moments the X-ray was done and I returned to the seats. After they made sure the films were fine, I could leave. I might have to return to orthopedics to learn about my X-rays.

We would go into the cafeteria and have a quick lunch and then to an elevator and down to the second floor. This is where you would leave the main building and go to plastic surgery. Outside a fast walk across the lawn to the door of the plastic surgery. It always seemed that the walk was very long, probably because it was up a small hill.

If Dr. Dingman was in surgery, you had better come up with something to read or play with or find someone to talk with who was also waiting. It meant that you were going to be there for a very long time. As I looked about the waiting room, there were so many others who had facial deformities. It was then that I began to feel that I was not totally alone. It was there that I also began to realize just how fortunate I was. So many of the others had more serious deformities or injuries than I did.

I was six years old, and I would eat whatever I wanted even

though I was unable to open my mouth correctly. I enjoyed eating whatever I was given; I especially loved apples. If I had ever choked on food I probably would have died. There would have been no way to reach the item. Now I take it for granted that I can open and close my mouth to eat. I never thought about choking as a child. I am sure that fear was with my parents all the time. I guess when I look back I was being watched over by God each time I placed food into my mouth.

Dr. Dingman would enter the room to examine me as the residents and interns would gather around and begin to listen. The room was always crowded with the medical personnel. Dr. Dingman would always greet my mother and they would have a short chat about how I was doing. After he completed my examination, the room would empty, just leaving my mother and me.

I was diagnosed with ankylosis of the right temporal mandibular joint, which would involve the development of my mandible.

Stop and look closely at your face in a mirror. We all have heard the saying he or she has his or her jaw. The mandible gives the face the form, which extends into the lower part of that face and this extends into the cheek areas. The bone structure of the face is what gives the appearance. If this area is deformed like mine was, the face's ability to grow will change and shift if it is not corrected either, possibly upward, which happened in my case.

Anchylosis of the temporomaxillary joint, preventing movement of the lower jaw, if occurring in childhood, leads to atrophy or want of proper development of the bone. As a result, the patient grows up with an immature chin, which causes a very conspicuous disfigurement. This was so in my case.

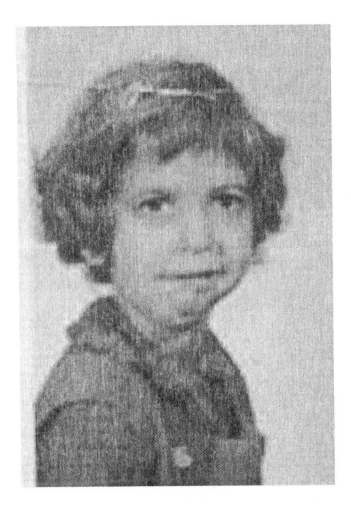

My face at age 6. 1964.

Turning his attention to me, Dr Dingman would ask me, "How is school going?" Then he would say, "Open your mouth." He always was interested in how the rest of my life was going. Dr. Dingman wore a headlight with a large eye flap, which he pulled down over his eye while turning on a very bright light to look into my mouth and examine my bite and teeth. During this time, young doctors twisted and turned to look into my mouth. Dr. Dingman began to explain my deformity to them as they took notes. I also listened. That is when I really began to learn about plastic surgery.

Dr. Dingman informed my mother that he had developed a procedure to release my TM joint. The decision was made to allow the surgery. Turning my head to the right side he pointed along side of my head and explained how he was going to perform a bone graft and release the right TM joint.

Dr. Dingman explained that if the graft did not work he would remove the bone in my little toe, for it was the same size as the TM joint, and would work the same way.

A picture was drawn to further explain where the graft was going to be taken from and how it was going to be placed. Drawing pictures would become part of explaining surgeries to me. It was decided that the surgery would be performed during the summer when school was out.

The date for surgery was set for August 16, 1965. I would be 7 at the time of the first surgery. I was sent back to X-ray, and a few X-rays of the cranial region were taken. It was late afternoon when we returned home with the news.

The months passed. I enjoyed the rest of the school year and the summer vacation before the surgery. It was early morning on that August day when my parents walked into my hospital room. There was not much talking going on. It was a hard time for them. It was not a hard time for me. Maybe I was too young to realize the seriousness of the surgery or maybe I just knew that I would soon be back in my second home—pediatrics. I felt comfortable there; the white coats did not scare me.

Soon the orderly came from surgery to take me down. I was placed onto a small stretcher, said goodbye, and headed for surgery.

After my arrival in the operating room there was much going on. Doctors and nurses were walking about with masks on their faces. Some of them spoke to me and let me know everything was going to be fine. The room was very cold with gray walls. There was a very large light that was pulled down over my face as my head was gently placed into position.

I kept looking for Dr. Dingman, and then he appeared. I guess I wanted to make sure he was there.

Dr. Dingman spoke through his mask. I could see his eyes. He explained that they were getting ready to put me to sleep. I watched as surgical tools were placed onto a green towel, which looked like a napkin. They were moved near the table. The table was very narrow. I remember shaking from the cold.

Dr. Dingman walked around the table talking with doctors and nurses. X-rays hung nearby. They began to move things around getting ready for the procedure. Then Dr. Dingman told me, "You are going to be put to sleep now." A black mask was placed over my nose and mouth. I felt like I was choking and I had the last memory of moving, trying to get the smell of ether away from my nose.

The surgery was many hours long. I returned to the recovery room feeling very ill from the ether that was used. For the first time in my life I was able to open my mouth. I read once that "God will do nothing without man. If God works a miracle, he does so through man." This was indeed a miracle!

I was very cold and nurses placed covers over me and talked

to me as I was trying to wake up. I could hear the nurse say, "Joy! Hello! You're in the recover room and doing just fine." I opened my eyes and looked around at nurses dressed in scrubs and walking about.

That was when I opened my mouth for the first time in my life! I did not even realize that I had done so.

Dr. Dingman spent over four years developing the surgical techniques used on my TM joint. My surgery was the first time these techniques were ever used in the history of plastic surgery. My facial deformity was so rare that Dr. Dingman had to develop special techniques.

At the time of his retirement, all of Dr. Dingman's cases were taken over by Dr. Argenta. Dr. Dingman wrote several articles and gave lectures about the surgeries he performed on me. At one time my case was used as a teaching tool at the University of Michigan.

This was the start of the reconstruction of my face. The nurse with me in recovery was very attentive—she never left my bedside, and if she did another nurse appeared. I was very ill and was unable to focus very well and would go in and out of consciousness. Each time the nurse would say, "Joy, you're doing well." She was watching all my vital signs. Then I looked toward the foot of the bed and there was Dr. Dingman. He smiled and gave a few instructions before leaving the area. I drifted in and out again. It was late evening when I was finally returned to pediatrics. I was still very sick from the ether.

I was in great pain along the side of my head and it hurt to turn my head to the right side. I was given pain medication to help the pain as I began to come around more.

By the next day things were much different. I was coming around and starting to sit up. I was opening and closing my mouth. I had pain but for some reason I wasn't allowing the pain to stop me. I was able to keep the bone in my little toe. For some reason I was worried that I had lost the bone in my little toe. I was greatly relieved that I still had the bone. I kept checking my feet to be absolutely sure. I did not realize how important my little toe had become to me.

Dr. Dingman was able to use the graft that was taken on the side of my head. The other joint performed well, and I only have one TM joint located on the left side. I could open my mouth and enjoy chewing food like other people. The food tasted better, and I decided at a young age that Dr. Dingman could repair anything.

It wasn't long until I was allowed, with the nurse's help, to start walking. Within a very short time the IV was taken out and I felt free. Each day there was much improvement. Children will always bounce back faster than adults will. I was healing and eating. I was only in the hospital for one week.

The large white bandage around my head and down under my jaw allowed support. I would look at myself in a mirror and touch the bandage. I sat in front of a mirror and opened and closed my mouth. I would look down into my mouth.

Aunt Geri and Uncle Benton came with gifts, and they stayed for several hours with me, giving my mother and father a break. As the years passed, my Aunt Geri would always be there just to help out whenever it was needed.

My older brother was overwhelmed when he first saw me after surgery. There was no swelling in the face, just a large bandage. I don't know what he expected to see. It was probably very scary to a 14-year-old. The appearance of the bandage did not bother me. I looked like a mummy but I could chew food like everyone else.

I was soon going up and down the hall of pediatrics. I had almost no pain. I played in the sunroom, stopping at a mirror and opening my mouth. I liked looking down this dark tunnel of my mouth. I though that was great. I observed my teeth and took a good look at my tongue and teeth. I could tell Dr. Dingman was very pleased with my recovery, and with the fact the surgery worked.

At night I looked out my hospital window, looking across into another wing. There was a man who would wave at me from a ward located in the other wing of the hospital, and I always waved back. One night I looked to wave and he was gone. I never got to say hello. I wondered who he was. I always wondered what happened to this man.

During the week, Dr. Dingman and groups of young doctors would come in to examine me. My stay was coming to an end.

One evening, late, I was at the pay phone with a dime to call home. My Uncle Thomas and Aunt Geneva turned the corner of the hall in pediatrics. My aunt was carrying a doll wearing purple feathers. I climbed down from the step stool, and we returned to my room. Nurses came in and out during their visit and each said how pretty my doll was. I kept the doll with the purple feathers for a long time. To this day I still do not know whatever happened to that doll.

Early the next morning Dr. Dingman let me know I was going home. He gave my mother instructions concerning my TM joint.

Dr. Dingman explained that my mother could allow me to have chewing gum now. That sounded great to a seven-year-old. He further explained how this would build up the muscles around the TM joint. He also explained that I would have to place tongue depressors in my mouth. This was a form of physical therapy to keep the joint working. The goal was to stack as many tongue depressors as possible in my mouth.

I was sent home a very happy seven-year-old with much to

look forward to. Now that I could open my mouth, the dental care began as permanent teeth were coming in but not straight. My bottom teeth were turned in and looking down my throat. The upper teeth were overlapping the lower jaw, causing the teeth to be bucked in the front. This further impaired my appearance. I was unable to close my mouth correctly. The mandible (lower jaw) would not match up with the maxillary (upper jaw). I was living in a world of people with normal faces. Did this cause emotional problems? No! I never developed emotional problems about being with people. Nor did I allow the remarks from other children to cause me to become a shut-in.

If I had not known that my face was going to be corrected, my life would have been a very different story. The following information is from my medical record concerning the TMJ surgery, dictated by Dr. Oneal:

Date, August 17, 1965. This seven-year-old female, at the age of 18 months, was found to have an abnormal growth of her mandible, and shortly after birth, she had an episode of septicemia. This may be related to the problem in her temporal mandibular joints. Follow-up examination: the growth in the right mandibular is very retarded. Growth on the left is not normal, but is more near normal than the right. Recent laminograms have shown a complete bony ankylosis of the right temporal mandibular joint, marked undergrowth of the right mandible, and there is also severe joint disease on the left side. A temporal mandibular joint arthroplasty was planned on the right side possibly metatarsal graft.

Procedure: The patient in the supine position and she had been intubated intra-nasally, because of inability to open mouth due to her ankylosed right temporal

Mandibular joint. A straight incision was made down the scalp into the periauricular area, avoiding the area of the lobule. Dissection was carried through skin and subcutaneous tissue, down to the temporal fascia. Various bleeders were clamped and ligated or electrocoagulated. The temporal fascia at the zygomatic arch was incised transversely and a large vein in this area was ligated and divided. By dissecting periosteum off the area of the condyle, the area of the joint was exposed, and essentially there was no joint exposed, and essentially there was no joint. There was a complete ankylosis. It would appear to be very flattened and abnormal condylar neck and head. There was essentially no normal notch or even choroid process, however, this area was not ankylosed. Consequently, using the bone drill, a cross cut was made about one-half centimeter below the...what normally would have been the glenoid fossa down through the outer table of this bone, which appeared to be somewhat softened and almost through the posterior table. The rest of this resection of this condylar head area was carried out, using an osteotome and a mallet. The bone was extremely thick in this area, being almost 1 centimeter thick, and the bone had to be removed in several fragments, and there was a moderate amount of bleeding from a venous plexus on the under surface of the condylar neck and head area. There was essentially no normal glenoid fossa and no articular cartilage in the area. Bleeding was controlled with pressure and Gelfoam and then a temporal muscle fascia flap was dissected in the area immediately above the zygomatic arch and turned down posteriorly and sutured into the area of the temporal mandibular joint. Following removal of this bone, there appeared to be reasonably adequate function and it was possible to open the mouth, making the supposition that the left temporal mandibular joint was probably better functioning than had been anticipated. Consequently, no exploration was carried out. A drain was placed into the fossa of the temporal mandibular joint on the right side, and the wound was closed in layers using 0000 chromic catgut, 0000 plain catgut, and 000000 Dermalon in the periauricular area, and 0000 Dermalon on the scalp. A pressure dressing was placed on the patient. Extubation was carried out successfully, and she returned to recovery room in good condition. Pack and sponge count was correct.... The estimated blood loss was 100 cc, no blood was replaced.

The University of Michigan Hospital during the 1960s.
Courtesy of Bentley Historical Library, Ann Arbor, Michigan.

Chapter 5
The Second Face Operation:
Building Out the Lower Jaw

In American society today, many people are having plastic surgery. Plastic surgery is very serious step. It should not be performed only for vanity. Many people who require plastic surgery are doing so because of a medical condition or an accident.

World War I plastic surgeons worked hard at repairing mandibles 50 years earlier. I am sure they would have been impressed at the work performed on my jaws. Many different techniques were developed and used during World War I.

Plastic surgery studies of the faces of different nationalities, especially the development of the cheekbones, were vital in the reconstruction of the mandible.

From studies of Native Americans, Asians and Caucasians, it was noted in a 1919 plastic surgery book the following information:

The malar bone, or zygomatic, make the prominence of the cheek, is attached to the zygoma of the temporal bone, and has a great deal to do with the shape of the face, as configuration of the cheek depends upon it. In normal configuration it varies much in different races. This can be easily appreciated by comparing the face of the North American Indian with that of an individual of the yellow or the white race.[23]

In July of 1969, with all the changes going on in the world around me, I would face a change that I had waited my childhood for. The dream that came true—a new face.

Dr. Dingman had been waiting for me to mature. He was also concerned about how I was being treated by others, especially children at school and in my neighborhood.

Dr. Dingman asked my mother, "Is Joy having problems with remarks at school?"

She replied, "She has her bad days but all in all things are good."

I will never know the hours spent in meetings concerning this one operation. I do know that Dr. Dingman was confidant that the operation was going to work, and that made me confident also.

I was 10 years old by the time the second surgery was decided. I had become a private patient of Dr. Dingman. From that period on, I would be seen at Dr. Dingman's private office. This office was located across the street from the Old St. Joseph Mercy Hospital in Ann Arbor on North Ingalls.

My second surgery was done on July 23, 1969, at St. Joseph Mercy Hospital. I was 11 years old by this time. A piece of my right hipbone was grafted into the right and left sides of my mandible, and the bone graft was wired into place. Drains were placed into the mandible area. (Refer to Dr. Dingman's notes that are located at the end of this chapter.) Again I was in the hospital only one week. The hip was very painful; I'm sure it was because I had put weight on it to walk. It was 3 days before I could put weight on my hip. The hip gave me more problems than my jaws and having them wired shut.

Many pictures were being taken, and studies were performed of my face. The orthodontist's job was to build a mold. This mold was a solid piece of acrylic that was placed into my mouth along with three wires to hold the jaws together until I healed. Weeks before the surgery I would visit the orthodontist, and he would have me bite into a mouthpiece with a pink substance within. After this would dry, they would begin to construct the mold that was going to be used.

On one visit the orthodontist showed me the plaster mold of my mouth which was developed into an acrylic structure. It was to be placed in my mouth during the surgery. For the 12 weeks following my surgery, I had to have that mold in my mouth.

Dr. Dingman took many different photographs to show my face at different angles. My teeth were also photographed to observe their location. For now, the main goal was to build out the face and match the upper and lower jaw. The pictures showed the shortness of the mandible. There were many measurements taken of my face. The bone graft was taken from the top of the right hip. Removing the graft did not cause any permanent injury and healed well.

In preparing for this kind of surgery, I learned from my orthodontist that the cut made in my jaws had to be made behind the bloodline. This protected my teeth. If the cut was in front of the bloodline, my teeth would receive damage for this was the blood supply to the teeth.

I entered St. Joseph Mercy Hospital on July 22, 1969. My ward was located at the end of the hallway in pediatrics. I watched as nuns walked up and down the halls in Pediatrics. The day went by fast and soon visiting hours were over and my parents left me. A nurse came in and handed me some Phisohex and explained I needed to wash my face and brush my teeth. I was never handed toothpaste. Looking at this green bottle in my hand, I went off to the bathroom. I washed my face and then placed this soap on my toothbrush, like an idiot, I actually brushed my teeth and became very ill. After I spit and spit and rinsed and rinsed I was okay. The smell of that soap even today will cause me to become ill.

On the way out of that bathroom, I stopped to look into the mirror at my old face for the last time. I knelt and I said a quiet little prayer. I never had fears about the surgery. I left the bathroom and the nurse asked if I had brushed my teeth. I smiled and said "yes" as I handed her back the green bottle of Phisohex soap.

I had 4 roommates that night. The roommates and I talked. Soon lights were turned off in the ward and I lay in bed and listened to the nurses going up and down the hallway as I slowly drifted off to sleep.

The next morning my parents were by my bed when an orderly came to take me to surgery. My mother kissed me goodbye. The cheerful orderly rolled me out into the hall and down to the elevator. I watched as the elevator doors opened and we went inside. I watched with him as the floor numbers lit up until we reached the operating room. The door opened and he moved me quickly into a room. Then I was moved to the operating room. I was placed on the operating table. Above my head were pictures of my face. They were hanging on thin wires. The operating room was a cold gray color with stainless steel sinks along one wall.

Dr. Dingman walked up, and as he spoke to me he smiled. Dr. Dingman observed the pictures over my head. I watched as he reviewed each one. Soon my arm was gently placed on a board and then tape was placed around my arm and an IV was started. I looked for Dr. Dingman. He was walking about the room getting things ready and talking with nurses and doctors. From a very small window I could see the American flag on top of the University of Michigan Hospital. I made a remark about the hospital. The nurse patted me on the leg and told me they were going to take very good care of me at St. Joe's.

Then Dr. Dingman told me I was going to be put to sleep. My head was placed in position. The last voice I heard was Dr. Dingman's. I would be in surgery for the next five long hours.

I woke up slowly in the recovery room as nurses stood by my bedside. I tried to open my mouth and it was then that I realized what wired jaws felt like. It was a strange feeling, like a key had locked the door, and no matter what I did it wasn't going to open. My mouth felt very full and I could feel the mold with my tongue. The mold was smooth, and I was able to swallow and turn my head. At this point I did not feel pain. I was having problems staying awake. A nurse raised my head to allow the pressure to be released on my face. They would talk to me and were checking my vital signs. I would try to respond to the nurses, but was having problems because of my jaws being wired shut.

Dr. Dingman and the other doctors came by to see how I was doing. I have a memory of Dr. Dingman saying my name. A nurse remained close to my bed after the doctors left. I was given shots in my left hip to relieve the pain that had begun to come. I gradually became somewhat more alert, but then I would drift off again.

At 7 p.m. I was returned to the floor, but I was not fully awake. I have almost no memory of the floor that night. The nurses kept coming in and I was given more pain medication. My parents and others were just blurs. My mother remained with me through the night. My mother was concerned because I couldn't make a sound. I also had an IV board on my right arm, and the buzzer for the nurses was on my right side.

One nurse was upset with my mother for staying with me through the night. The next morning Dr. Dingman asked my mother if she had any problems. She replied "no" then Dr. Dingman told my mother that he had talked to the Mother Superior. Mother Superior had said that my mother was welcome to stay as long as she wanted. Dr. Dingman understood her fears. He too was a parent. My room was located at the end of the hallway far from the nurses' station. Even if I was able to make a sound or if I became ill or choked I had no way of getting help from the nurses.

The next evening my mother was given a blanket and a pillow, and there were no more problems concerning her staying in my room. My mother remained two nights with me. My Aunt Geri stayed one night, to allow my mother a break.

When I was able to reach and call the nurse, I no longer required my mother or my aunt at night. I walked down the hall with the assistance of the nurse and was bouncing back and showing improvements. I had drainage tubes under my jaws to keep fluids from building up. In order for me to breathe, I had to be frequently suctioned. That was horrible and very painful.

I wanted to look at my face and was given a mirror to take a look. It was very different I was not that swollen, and surprisingly I was not that black and blue. I just had a small amount of swelling under my new jaw line. I was very pleased as I looked into the mirror that day.

I was placed on a total liquid diet, which was a lot of chicken broth and milk shakes. I looked forward to the milk shakes. The milk shakes would have many nutrients mixed in. One ingredient was a raw egg and a spoonful of iron. I was given much iron to take, and this was to build my blood back.

Dr. Dingman, along with many doctors, would make rounds, and I would listen to every word being said. I remember there were times Dr. Dingman would make rounds very late. I would wake up because I could hear them speaking in what they thought were low tones. I always knew that Dr. Dingman was very busy and sometime during the day or evening I would see him. I would often see the residents and interns, and I watched how they would take notes and asked questions. This was a real learning experience for all concerned, and what they learned they carried on in their practices.

I was released from St. Joseph Hospital after being there for only seven days. At home I often would sit in a chair and cover myself with a blanket. I began to have cravings for good food. My mother would fix dinner, and I could sit and smell the food in the living room. She would fix me some broth and bring it out to me. I would look at it, and she would return with a milk shake and liquid Keflex. I loved spinach and we had a blender so my mother took some spinach and ran it through the blender until it was soup. I could get that into a straw and that was heaven.

She added a little salt—that was a big treat. She learned how to run a few good tasting items through the blender and it made life much better. I drank a lot of different Campbell's soups. I became an expert on the different types of soup during that period. I would sleep sitting straight up because that would relieve pressure on my face. My brother thought I wasn't resting. He was very concerned about that.

After a few weeks at home, my mother and I decided to go shopping in town. I was feeling very good and we thought getting out of the house would be a fun time. It was very hot and humid that day. I got sick and almost passed out on her. I was taken inside Cunningham's Drug Store. Because they had air conditioning, I soon was fine. Mother took me home where I rested, and things soon became normal. I was still a little weak.

After about 3 weeks, I began to play outside with friends. School was starting soon, and I was going into the sixth grade. My jaws were still wired closed when I started back to school. I walked to and from school each day. My jaws remained wired until November; it was a long 12 weeks. It was not long after that until my teacher could understand me. I would take a thermos to school with soup and have my lunch just like the others with no problem.

Because Dr. Dingman was in surgery, Dr. Oneal had to remove the wires. Dr. Oneal was having some problems; I was unable to relax. He removed the first wire, and I heard the bone crack. Dr. Oneal gave me a break and spoke with my mother. After awhile I was able to relax, the wires were removed, and I was fine. I would have had the same problem no matter who removed the wires. I did much better when I was older and knew what to expect.

I had become a pack rat. I took home with me the wires and mold. I kept them for years in a locked box, and I would show them to friends. I often sat in the quietness of my room and examined them. I don't know why I kept them in a locked box. No one was going to take them.

I think that all patients who are going to have their jaws wired shut should have a nice steak dinner the night before. It will be a long time before they get a really good meal. Not everyone likes liquefied spinach.

After this surgery on my jaws, the next step was to put braces on my teeth. This began when I was 14, which was the earliest possible time.

I became interested in the history of orthodontics. I found the following quotes about its history to be of interest:

> Teeth-straightening and extraction to improve alignment of remaining teeth has been practiced since early times. Orthodontics, as a science of its own, did not exist until the 1880s. [24]

> This field of dentistry was developed, and by 1728 writings were being published by Pierre Fauchard (1678–1761). It was a French dentist, Bourdet, who followed Fauchard in 1757, with his book *The Dentist's Art* concerning the alignment of teeth and appliances to be used. The causes and treatment of dental irregularities were dealt with for the English speaking world in a book written by John Hunter in 1771 titled *The Natural History Of Human Teeth*.[25]

> Time marched on and more interested was developed. By 1841 the term orthodontia was coined by Lafoulon along with publication of a book by J.M. Alexis Schange on malocclusion— the abnormal fitting of the teeth in upper and lower jaws. Then in 1858, Dr. Normal W. Kingsley in his 1880 *Treatise on Oral Deformities*, began to expand the field making Kingsley the father of orthodontics. J.N. Farrar wrote two volumes concerning *A Treatise on the Irregularities of the*

Teeth and Their Corrections. Farrar developed many methods to move teeth. He is referred to as the father of modern orthodontics. The third influential figure in orthodontics was Edward H. Angle (1855–1930). Angle designed orthodontic appliances and was the founder of the first school and college of orthodontia. He organized the American Society of Orthodontia in 1901 and in 1907 published the first orthodontic journal."[26]

My teeth were braced in 1973. I had four teeth removed in oral surgery. I was volunteering at University of Michigan at the time. I visited oral surgery, and a young doctor removed two teeth. He said, "That is it for today."

I replied, "No, get the other two also. One big hurt is better than two little ones." He thought a moment and decided to remove the other two teeth.

I had no problem, and two days later I ran into him as I was going into Mott's Children's Hospital to do my volunteer work. He looked shocked that I was okay. I did not have any pain and no swelling and was glad that problem was over.

I wore braces on my teeth until 1976. On one visit to the orthodontist, I asked him if I was ever going to get the braces off. He explained to me that my teeth moved very fast, and to make sure that they would remain in place I had to wear the braces longer. They were removed in the summer of 1976, after my senior year in high school. I had to attend my senior prom with braces on my teeth.

In March of 1969, Dr. Dingman's notes refer to my models being gone over with the orthodontist. The following drawings and photos of my jaws follow this chapter.

REED O. DINGMAN, M.D.
Plastic and Reconstructive Surgery

DATE...

NAME......LOVE, Miss Joy.................................ADDRESS...

AGE............OCCUPATION...PHONE...................................

REFERRING DOCTOR..ADDRESS..............................

CHIEF COMPLAINT...

HISTORY: 10-2-64 continued:
X-rays will be gotten at the time of her next visit and the surgery
planned. (SP) *Right condylectomy - c̄ Temporal muscle flap*
3-17-65 inserted into space.
3-26-69: Doctor   and I have gone over her models and we feel that a bilateral
osteotomy with bilateral bone grafts to the mandible would be the best course to follow
EXAMINATION: in this case. Doctor   will make splints of clear acrylic to fit on the teeth. Iliac
bone grafts will be used to fill in the bone defect. (D)

Left   *Right*

12 mm   *26 mm*

Bilateral osteotomy of mandible
with iliac bone grafts.

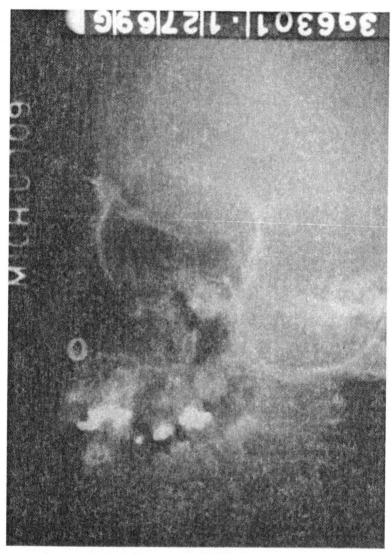

Joy Love's face X-ray, 1969, at age 11.

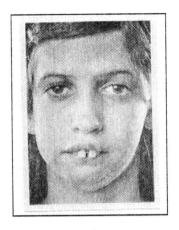
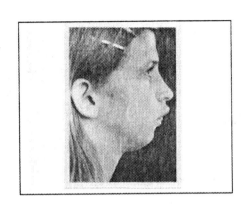
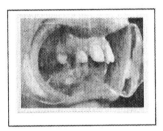
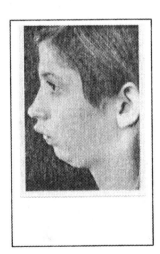
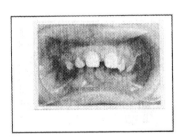

1969 at age 11. Pictures of face and teeth taken before surgery by
Dr. Reed O. Dingman.

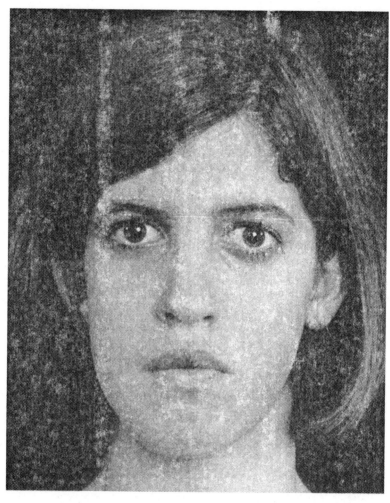

1971 Picture taken by Dr. Reed O. Dingman at age 12 after the surgery.

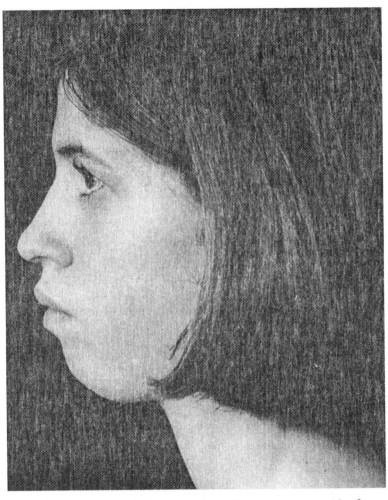

1971 picture taken by Dr. Reed O. Dingman at age 12 after the surgery.

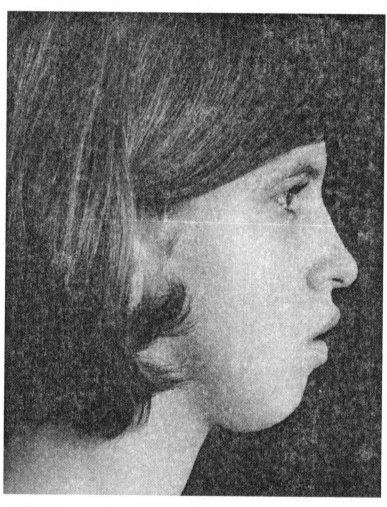

1971 Picture taken by Dr. Reed O. Dingman at age 12 after the surgery.

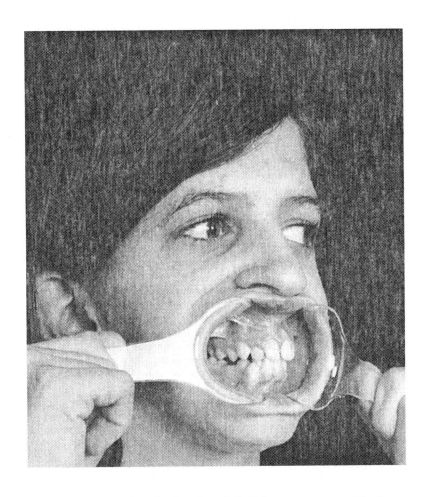

1971 Picture taken by Dr. Reed O. Dingman at age 12 after the surgery.

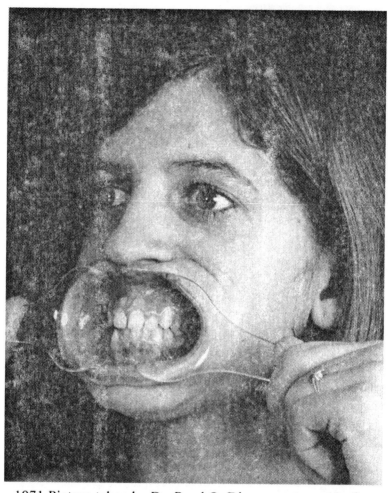

1971 Picture taken by Dr. Reed O. Dingman at age 12 after the surgery.

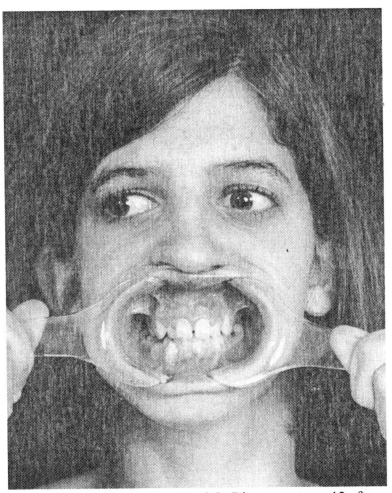

1971 Picture taken by Dr. Reed O. Dingman at age 12 after the surgery.

St. Joseph Mercy Hospital in Ann Arbor, Michigan, as it looked in 1969.
Photo courtesy of St. Joseph Mercy Hospital archives.

Chapter 6
Osteotomy of Symphysis, Maxilla and Nasal Obstruction

On a visit with Dr. Dingman, in 1977, he checked my mandible and we talked about the midline to the right side of my face. I did not have enough chin, and it was decided to enhance my chin. This was to me a very minor operation and very fast recovery. This was referred to as a symphysis osteotomy, using cartilage taken from a cartilage box. I was nineteen at the time of this operation.

One June 23, 1977, the cartilage implant was placed on the left side of the mandible. There was still a tiny bit of flatness along the border of the mandible. I was very happy with the work done. I recovered in a very short time and was looking forward to attending the University of Alabama. The following was taken from my medical chart of Dr. Dingman's notes concerning my surgery:

On June 23, 1977, surgery—mandibular symphysis osteotomy and advancement and cartilage implant to left side of the body of the mandible. On June 30, 1977, condition excellent. August 4, 1977, condition excellent. She has slight flatness along the left border of the mandible. The result today is quite satisfactory. To return in 6 to 8 months. Photographs taken today.

The maxilla was a harder operation. I was not able to completely close my mouth. My upper lip did not match up with the lower lip without great effort on my part, and I was unable to hold my mouth closed. Dr. Dingman had not noticed this, but after he saw what the problem was, he was able to decide how to correct the problem.

At first we talked about possibly making the upper lip longer to give a better appearance. This idea was discussed and a decision was finally reached. Dr. Dingman had a meeting with my orthodontist. It was decided that the entire maxilla would be moved in an upward position to decrease the height of the mid-facial dimension. This did not require any type of bone graft. It would be an excision of approximately 5–7 millimeters of tissue to permit decrease in the vertical dimension. The orthodontist made models that were going to be put into place during the surgery.

On February 10, 1982, I was taken into surgery again at St. Joseph Mercy Hospital in Ann Arbor. The surgery lasted four hours. During this surgery I began to bleed, and the location of the bleeding was unknown. Dr. Dingman reported to my parents that he almost lost me. There was not a bleeder cut during this surgery. It still remains a mystery as to where the blood came from and how the bleeding stopped.

I awoke in recovery and was shaking very hard. I received two units of blood in the operating room. I was having a very hard time in recovery and remained in recovery for a long while. My mouth was again wired closed. I had hopes that this could have been done without my mouth being wired, but due to the work performed it was a must.

I returned to the floor feeling good and was doing well. I still was shaking and cold, but in time it slowed down and things were fine.

I had a small device placed into my nose I called a bugle. The first two nights things were going well. I had a new nurse taking care of me and I began to hyperventilate, and it scared me. For some reason I decided to have my mother called, not Dr. Dingman. The nurse called my home.

It was after midnight. We lived only two miles from the hospital. As my mother was coming down the hall, she met Dr. Dingman on the floor. He asked her why she was there, and she told him. They both came to my room, and there I sat. The nurse and I were totally lost as to what was happening to me. We were both just scared. I was her first patient to have their mouth wired shut. Dr. Dingman reached over and removed the bugle from my nose and smiled at the young nurse and me. He then backed up and asked me if I could breath. I explained I could. He had a twinkle in his eye. I laughed later. I should have asked for him to begin with and I think he probably wondered why I had my mother called. I was not at all in danger.

Dr. Dingman left for a trip, and I was left in the care of another doctor. My orthodontist would come during the day and sit by my bedside. I often opened my eyes and could see him quietly sitting by my bed. After a few days I was released to go home. It was then I began to shake very badly and I was unable to control the shaking. I was unable to sleep, sit, or eat. I had never experienced anything like it. I was soon taken to the ER, and on the way I was nauseous. I was quickly cared for. I remained overnight. It was later learned that I was possibly going into surgical shock. After that everything was placed under control. I began to stop shaking and was released. We will never know what caused that and it will remain a mystery.

The next few weeks I lost a lot of weight, but I was in general good health, and when the wires were removed had no problem regaining the lost weight. Dr. Dingman asked me if I drank beer; I said yes. He told me to drink one beer a day to help put the weight back on. What a treat to have a beer to go with my soup. That was the best prescription I ever got.

After my maxillary surgery, I was determined to return to Eastern Michigan University. During winter term of 1982, I took my oral exams while wired shut and did not miss a lecture. I finished and graduated in May of 1982, with a Bachelor of Science degree in history. I never allowed my surgery to hold me back. I felt that getting back into the mainstream of life was a part of healing. I missed my friends and just being out in the world. Surgery is just a minor setback

I would visit Dr. Dingman's office and we would talk about my education and what I was planning to do. He truly was interested in me personally and in my well-being. I learned from listening to him how a true professional acted. I have letters from him and received countless words of advice. I always enjoyed visiting with Dr. Dingman's nurses. I had known some of them since my early childhood. Ours was a special bond.

When Dr. Dingman became ill, I remember going to visit with him during his stay at St. Joseph Mercy Hospital. I had gone out of town for Christmas Eve in 1985. When I returned home I received a phone call that Dr. Dingman had passed away.

I lost a true friend. I had admired him my entire life. Dr. Dingman left the field of plastic surgery a legend. Dr. Dingman's work allowed the University of Michigan to be one of the top plastic surgery departments in the nation and known internationally.

Many developments in plastic surgery were made by Dr. Dingman and passed to younger doctors. His books and articles will be reviewed for years to come. I was honored to have known him.

He made a lasting impression on anyone's life that he touched. He was man of his word. Dr. Dingman's name is known both nationally and internationally, and I am sure his kind heart is well remembered.

Dr. Dingman developed tools to be used during plastic surgery. I often think that in 30 years from now as young surgeons pick up one of those tools, it's too bad they won't know the man who invented them. I missed hearing his voice coming down a hallway and will always remember his smile.

Doctor Reed O. Dingman's name is remembered within the Reed O. Dingman Society, which has many members. The Reed O. Dingman Award is given to top plastic surgeons throughout the world.

After Dr. Dingman's death, I became a patient of Dr. Louis Argenta, who was trained by Dr. Dingman. Today Dr. Argenta works in Wake Forest University as a plastic surgeon.

I had noticed that my nose had begun to move sideways in 1985, and that I was having severe sinusitis problems. I decided to return for further plastic surgery.

After a short chat with Dr. Argenta, he examined my nose. He discovered that I was unable to breathe correctly. I had a nasal obstructed airway and a deviated septum with a sinus infection. Dr. Argenta decided to repair the problem. It was learned that I had a large floor spur and clouding of my maxillary sinus. This was a minor operation. When I recovered, this was the last operation I have had in plastic surgery in Ann Arbor, Michigan.

I have known Dr. Robert Oneal my entire life. Dr. Oneal always was interested in my case. He too is a special person to me. Dr. Oneal practices at St. Joseph Mercy Hospital in Ann Arbor, Michigan, and Saline Community Hospital in Saline, Michigan. Dr. Oneal was trained by and worked with Dr. Dingman.

Before his death, Dr. Dingman traveled the world to help countless children and adults by repairing facial disfigurements. There are many other surgeons who dedicate countless hours to perform plastic surgery for people in regions of the world where it is impossible to reach surgical teams of this kind. One such group known today is Smile Train. They travel the world helping children by repairing their cleft palates. Thanks to the surgeons and all the people that make these trips possible, smiles are brought to many children around the world. Visit Smile Train's web page and learn about their work.

Dr. Reed O. Dingman.
Courtesy of Bentley Library University of Michigan Ann Arbor,
Michigan.

Chapter 7
Hip and Knee/Sternum/Right Ventricular Shunt

The formal beginning of orthopedic surgery was in 1741 with Nicolas Andry (1658–1742) in Paris, France. Andry wrote a book that was translated into English. The book was titled *L'Orthopedie*. Andry derived the word *orthopedic* from Greek, *ortho* meaning straight and pais, meaning child. Many historians did not give acknowledgment to Andry. Andry was ahead of his time. He wrote fundamental information on subjects such as curvature of the spine, clubfeet, and congenital deformities. Andry was the first to note the active participation of muscles in producing deformities of the skeletal system. In 1685, Andry received a degree of Master of Arts, and up to 1690 he remained an ecclesiastic. Andry studied medicine at Rheims and Paris. He received a degree in medicine in 1697, at the age of 39.[27]

The ancient people's developments concerning injuries and

old age were the beginnings of orthopedics. Their methods and materials were very crude. They used any materials they could locate in nature, such as sticks, bamboo, grasses, and the like to make splits to repair fractures. Grasses and later ropes were tied around the fracture until the bone healed. The results were not always good. Mainly because of the type of fracture, many died due to infection.

The British were early explorers in methods used in orthopedics. They made much advancement from 1500–900. During this period, Europeans were also working on different methods and ideas concerning orthopedics. Many of the early Europeans left countless writings in medical books of their research and advancements in the field.

Wilhelm Conrad Rontgen discovered X-rays in 1895. His discovery and developments allowed the medical field to view the human body with pictures before deciding what measures had to be taken to repair the problem. It was invaluable to be able to view a fracture or deformity. That was a great tool for orthopedic surgery.

By the 1900s, Americans were making advancements in the field of orthopedics; in doing so many contributions were being made. In 1940 Dr. Austin T. Moore of South Carolina researched and developed, and then performed the first total hip replacement in the world.

A hip deformity throws the entire body off balance and will cause pain in many areas such as the back and shoulders. I have been very lucky. I have had very little back problems and this is due to controlling my weight.

On September 21, 1959, I was taken to the University of Michigan for a routine checkup. My mother thought I was a healthy baby by then and I had no signs otherwise. My older brother was trying to teach me to walk by placing me against the wall and saying, "Come on, baby," while holding out his arms. I was trying to take steps but not advancing like I should have been. My mother noticed that I was dragging my left leg. On this visit to the clinic she explained to a young doctor what I was doing. He quickly examined my hips and legs. It was late in the day. He told my mother that even though X-ray was closed he had a friend working in X-ray who would do the X-ray for him. He took me to X-ray. When he returned he told my mother that the X-ray showed a congenital dislocation of the left hip and that I should remain overnight.

On September 22, 1959, I was taken to the operating room. I was placed under general anesthesia, however no surgery was performed. During this time the doctors and several observers palpated my left hip. The anesthesia was so that I would not hurt during this procedure. After the procedure it was decided that with manipulation, the hip could be reduced readily. The head of the femur was easily palpable through the buttock on examination at this time, therefore probably ruling out the possibility of congenital absence of the head of the femur or a pyogenic infection of the femoral head. Following the reduction of the femur, I was placed in a spica cast (better known as a body cast). I did well and I returned home the next day. I remained in the body cast for about 3 months.

My next door neighbor, Julie Johnson, remarked to me once that I was like a little turtle as I moved about the floor pulling my body cast to reach whatever I wanted to. I wore the belly of the cast out. It was believed that the Serratia marcescens could have begun in the hip. Where it truly began in the bone will never be known. It was noted by orthopedics that I was developing normally and was very active. They noted that I had an excellent gait although there is a positive Trendelenberg on the left. I walked with a slight external rotation of the left foot.

Examination revealed the following range of motion: the flexors from 180 degrees of extension to 45 degrees of full flexion comparable to the opposite side. I had no internal rotation. External rotation was approximately 20 degrees. Abduction (outward rotation of the hip) is 60 degrees and adduction (inward rotation of the hip) is 40 degrees. At that time there was a 3/8-inch true leg length shorting on the left leg. The above range of motion of the hip is painless. There was moderate crepitus and mild instability when putting the hip through a range of motion.

My orthopedic doctor explained to my mother that in time the right leg could be pinned to slow the growth down. There would have been a pin surgically placed in the thighbone of my right leg to stunt the growth. This would allow the left leg to grow at a more even pace and would lessen the lift with age. Unfortunately this procedure was never done. It possibly would help have helped my back and shoulder alignment. I feel that playing and exercising the leg was helpful for the surgeries that were going to come.

I was placed under the new head of orthopedics. As I grew and reached the age of 12, I was having much pain in the left hip. I was sounding like a broken record complaining, and all that was being done were X-rays and medication. I felt like the doctor did not believe that I was really hurting. It got to the point that I was often in the ER with lots of pain. I only wish that the "pinning procedure" could have been done years earlier. It might have saved me years of pain and discomfort, not to mention possible surgery.

Finally, this came to an end. A young doctor examined me in ER and informed my mother that something had to be done. He found that a jagged bone in my hip was the cause of my pain. He made a note in my chart for my surgeon to see.

In 1972, at age 13, my records moved to a different orthopedic doctor. He worked at St. Joseph Mercy Hospital. I was in such pain that when I walked you could hear the bone click inside of the left hip. I could neither sit nor stand, and it was very painful. He reviewed the X-rays and informed my mother that something had to be done. He studied the problem and decided how to correct the problem.

I was in the ninth grade when it was decided to remove the piece of bone that was jagged and hitting the pelvic bone. It was making the clicking sound when I walked or sat. My school nurse could hear me clicking as I walked. On the second day in ninth grade I was in such pain that the nurse sent me to the counselor and he called my mother to come and get me. I was in great pain. I could not sit or walk.

I had a hip surgery on December 28, 1972, at St. Joseph Mercy Hospital. It took several months to schedule my surgery. The jagged bone was removed and the hip was wired. He also clipped a small tendon on the inside of my leg. It really helped me to have more freedom of movement. It has not hurt since the surgery.

I remained in traction for about 3 weeks and in a body cast for 3 months. I was able to move about my home in a body cast without any problems. I had a homebound teacher for the 3 weeks in traction and 3 months I was in a body cast. When I returned to school for the last six weeks of my ninth grade year, I had no work to do. I had completed the balance of the year's work while I was at home. My math teacher found something for me to do.

It was worth all the trouble. After I was out of my cast, my friends gave me a surprise birthday party and we all had a good time. For the next 20 years I was free of pain in the left hip.

I had one more surgery performed by this orthopedic doctor.

Due to the way I walked, the right knee could no longer stand the pressure. I had gone tobogganing and fell on the ice. I think that after the fall is where some of the knee problem began. The doctor told my parents that my walking, which put more pressure on my right knee, could have torn the cartilage in the right knee. The torn cartilage was removed in 1973.

On November 30, 1974, I had to have my sternum shaved off flush. This problem may have been caused from me having to walk on crutches. This placed much pressure onto my sternum area, causing pain. A thoracic surgeon performed the surgery at St. Joseph Mercy Hospital. I was having much pain and it became inflamed. The surgeon confirmed that my extended use of crutches for almost 2 years started this problem. I also had very bad bruises under my arms. I finally learned to walk correctly using the crutches. I really wanted to get off of the crutches. Maybe a wheelchair at home would have been much better.

In my thirties, after years of working and standing on my legs, I began to have pain. The wire was no longer working. It was getting to the point that I was unable to get up and down and in and out of a car without pain. By this time I was developing severe arthritis, and the cold winters in Michigan were taking their toll. I had also had several bad falls on the ice getting around. I am very surprised that I did not break anything.

The hip was a very difficult hip to replace. My earlier orthopedist had passed away, and his partner was seeing me. The partner referred me to another orthopedic doctor at St. Joseph Mercy Hospital who he felt could perform the surgery.

After this orthopedic doctor examined me, he decided that I needed a total hip replacement. This was done under an epidural anesthetic on August 11, 1992. I was able to see the old hip when it was removed. I had decided I wanted to see what was causing me so much pain. It looked like the end of a beat-up baseball bat. My left leg was lengthened, and I no longer wear a lift on my left shoe. I think that they agreed to the epidural in part because of the bad reaction I had after the maxillary surgery. I had the shakes after that surgery; there was some fear that it might reoccur. I had no problem with the epidural.

The left leg that always turned outward was fixed, and after the surgery the left knee turned inward. This was because of the way the bone in the left leg grew. I walk with some unsteadiness today and sometimes with the assistance of a cane. The total hip is well placed, but I know that in time it too will be replaced with a new model.

Neurosurgery's beginnings date back to the ancient people including the early European, Egyptian, Indian, and South American Indian cultures, amongst others. They practiced the art of trepanation, which involved drilling holes in the head to release "evil spirits" or "bad humors." There is evidence that some of the people recovered and lived for years after that procedure. This is found on skulls from that period.[28]

Records of medical lore related to neurosurgery can be found in artifacts left by the ancient Sumerians and Egyptians.[29]

The nineteenth century allowed major advancements in surgery, making neurosurgery possible. Lord Joseph Lister developed antisepsis (bacteria-killing solution) along with asepsis (sterile technique), and these reduced infection. The development of anesthesia by William T.G. Morton reduced the problem of pain and allowed more delicate surgery to be performed. The name Lister might be familiar to many of us who use Listerine.[30]

In the nineteenth century, "Great Britain's Sir Victor

Horsley became the first surgeon to specialize largely in Neurological Surgery. In the United States, Harvey Cushing, working beneath the famous William Halsted, became the first U.S. surgeon to dedicate his practice entirely to neurosurgery." Dr. Cushing became the father of modern neurosurgery.[31]

The first recorded reference to the nervous system is found in ancient Egyptian records. The Edwin Smith Surgical Papyrus, a 1700 B.C. copy of a manuscript composed about 3500 B.C., contains the first to use the word brain along with the description of the coverings of the brain and the fluids beneath them. Pythagoras, it is known, taught that the brain was concerned with reasoning. His pupil Alcmaeon performed the earliest known dissection of the human body (sixth century B.C.), and devoted some attention to the nervous system by discovering the optic nerves. In the fifth century B.C., Anaxagoras of Athens maintained that there was some relation between the peripheral nerves and the brain, and further asserted that the brain was the organ of the mind and the seat of the soul as well as the origin of the nerves.[32]

With the advent of Hippocrates (460–370 B.C.), diseases of the brain were recognized as being within the overall concept of medicine, and an ancient clinical descriptive neurology was born.... Hippocrates noted that man's brain resembled that of all other animals in being cleft into two symmetrical halves by a vertical membrane. Furthermore he observed that many blood vessels connect the brain; some are slender, but two are stout.[33]

During this period, Hippocrates made great steps in his discoveries and his writings. He wrote the remarkable tract *On the Sacred Disease*, about 400 B.C.[34]

As a people, we greatly owe these ancient pioneers for they opened the door that gave men and women physician's knowledge to learn more in the field of neurology.

I have two memories of events that took place that might have led to the beginnings of my headaches. Our family had gone on a camping trip in Upper Michigan. It was during that trip I had a strange feeling like I was being shocked. That feeling began in one side of my head and it seemed to travel through my entire body. This feeling lasted for just brief moments and disappeared, and I felt normal again. My parents decided that we needed to go back home.

About six months later I was taken to St. Joseph Mercy Hospital. My right arm felt like I had placed my finger into an electric outlet. My fingers were tingling and hurting. After being examined, my arm was put into a sling. It was thought that I had damaged a nerve in my elbow. The sling did no good. The cause of the pain was not found, and in time this too disappeared.

I still have some episodes of this type of pain. I feel that the damage probably was done during this time. No one has ever determined the cause of the pain. There must be some damage somewhere in the brain that is causing this pain.

During the eleventh grade of high school when I was 17, I began to develop headaches. There was no apparent reason. The pain would begin on the right side of my head. It would progress across the top of my head to the left temple region.

They began as very low grade and as the day would continue, the pain would sometimes increase. Most of the headaches would be followed with severe nosebleeds that were very difficult to stop most of the time. The headaches lasted from 1975 until July of 1980 when the cause was finally found, and I had brain surgery to relieve the cranial pressure. During all this time of trying to find the cause and cure of the headaches, I was prescribed no medication. I think that the doctors were concerned about possible side effects of pain relievers.

I went to the Neurosurgery Department at the University of Michigan Hospital in 1975. Many causes were suggested, nothing was found, and the headaches continued during 1976, my last year of high school. The headaches continued throughout the fall term of college in 1976.

The pain was sometimes severe. I would go to my classes at Washtenaw Community College and have difficulties trying to read the board because of the severe pain. Noise from radios, TVs, or just normal daily types of noises caused the pain to intensify. Certain lights like TVs and car lights at night caused the pain to intensify. This made taking notes in class extremely difficult. There were times that I had double vision. The headaches often caused dizziness.

These problems affected me in many different ways. I would become depressed with the continuous pain. I began to believe that no one understood what was wrong. (At that time no one did know the cause of the problem.) I thought that some people felt that I was really in no pain, that it was psychosomatic or that I was a hypochondriac. I was being sent to many different departments at the University of Michigan from the Headache Clinic to ENT, the works. I began to feel like a ping-pong ball.

I had a brain scan at the University of Michigan. The scan did not reveal the problem. Other doctors from other departments were trying to discover the cause of the severe headaches, to no avail. The cause would remain hidden for another year.

I started college at the University of Alabama in the fall of 1978. I enjoyed going to school there. I lived in Adams Parker Dorm in Tuscaloosa. I became involved with Campus Crusade and enjoyed going to events on campus. That year Alabama was National Champions in football. The headaches became worse and the nosebleeds returned. I visited an eye doctor who thought that I should try wearing prisms on the lenses of my glasses. He thought the weak muscle in the left eye, the lazy eye, could be causing the pain. That made some sense but the problem wasn't going away.

Once, during an English class, my nose began to bleed so badly I had to remove myself to a bathroom where it took most of the class period to stop the bleeding. I returned and was able to listen to the last 10 minutes of the lecture. The professor was very concerned. He did not know what had happened to me.

I returned home for summer break and had the muscle in my left eye tied. This was performed by an ophthalmologist at St. Joseph Mercy Hospital in Ann Arbor, Michigan, on June 20, 1979. The ophthalmologists thought that by tying the muscle of my lazy eye might stop the headaches. The surgery did help my double vision for about one month. But it did not help the headaches!

I returned to school in the fall of 1979. I was still having severe headaches. This time the headaches were becoming much worse than before. I was unable to focus on my studies due to the pain. I then knew that the lazy eye wasn't the problem.

I did manage to finish the semester and returned home still

having the headaches off and on. This was still affecting my personality.

One afternoon during that fall semester, I was returning back to my dorm and was in such pain that after reaching my dorm I lay down and went into a deep sleep. I woke up with a severe nosebleed. It was at that time that I finally began to connect the nosebleeds to headaches and pressure.

After a few more days of this, I contacted my parents and I withdrew from the University of Alabama. My mother flew to Alabama and she drove us back to Michigan. I knew something was wrong with me. And I knew that something had to be done!

When I returned home I enrolled at Washtenaw Community College. After finishing that semester, I transferred to Eastern Michigan University to finish my degree. It was at this time that I returned back to the University of Michigan Hospital trying to get some relief from the headaches and to locate the problem that was causing them. Again I was sent to different departments until I felt neglected. I felt that I was getting shuffled from one department to another with no one really knowing what to do for me. This continued for several more months.

During the winter term of 1980, I could no longer take the constant pain. I decided to see a neurosurgeon who was rated very high in neurosurgery at St. Joseph Mercy Hospital.

I explained that my headaches were like eating ice cream too fast. That is how they would begin. On a CAT scan, with the use of dye, he found that I had hydrocephalus. I thought that the fluid was going to be removed with a needle. That is not what happened. I soon learned that they would place a shunt in the right ventricle of my brain to draw off the excess fluid. The surgery was performed about 30 days after the cause was determined.

When I was taken into surgery, it was found that I had intra-cranial pressure of 210 millimeters of mercury. This was double what it should have been for a 22-year-old person. A ventricular atrial shunt was placed into the right ventricle of my brain. The other end of the shunt was placed through an artery into my heart. My heart actually pumps the shunt. One thing I know for sure is that in time I would have had a stroke and that would have possibly ended my life if I had not had the shunt.

Before my surgery, Dr. Dingman was in pre-op with a patient and saw me. He looked shocked to see me there. I have always remembered how he took a chair and sat down with me until I was taken to surgery. We talked, and I could tell he was very concerned about me. I had never told Dr. Dingman about the headaches. I remember thinking how he took his valuable time to sit with me.

This was a very hard operation and the recovery was even harder. I received excellent care during my stay in the hospital. I have some vague memories of family and friends who visited with me.

I remember one evening I was having such problems that nurses were coming in and out checking me. A lot of the time while I was recovering from this surgery is a blur.

I remained in the hospital for a week and slowly began to regain my strength. I had major problems trying to walk down the hall even with the aid of a nurse. I was unable to walk straight. I felt like I did not have any strength and I wanted to remain in bed. I knew I had to get up no matter what and try to move around. In time, I was able to move about the hospital room. It was going to take awhile before I felt stable again.

I could not hear out of my right ear and it was like I was under water. The doctor explained to me that the feeling would go away and it did within a week.

I was finally having a good morning and was trying to watch television. The weather reported storms moving through the area. I was located on the sixth floor, the top floor of the hospital. Within a few hours the hospital was hit with a wind over 100 miles per hour and the nurses were moving us into the halls.

A nurse came in and asked me if I was able to walk. I told her "yes," and we walked to the nurse's desk. I called the storm the green thing because the sky was green and it howled so loud. I had just been given a pain shot so I did not fully appreciate the danger that we were in at the time.

The lights flickered on the floor and the nurses did very well at keeping everyone calm. I knew they were scared. This lasted for what seemed like an hour, leaving damage all the way to Detroit.

My mother was in the basement of our home as the wind ripped through the neighborhood. It ripped out a column from our house and knocked down trees. Mother was very concerned about me there at the hospital.

One scary thing I remember was the weatherman was forced to leave the station and was no longer able to broadcast due to the raging storm. There were countless theories about that storm. After it left the area, it became very hot and muggy outside. This was in July; it was not our normal weather happening.

I returned to Eastern Michigan University in the fall of 1980. I really had problems getting back into my college work. I felt like I had to relearn some things, like writing. I had to learn to concentrate again. I had problems taking notes and problems with retaining information from the lectures. With much hard work, things began to fall into place. This was only 2 months after my surgery.

After my return to college, I could study and have a good time again with friends and family without a headache. In time I began to heal, and the world became worth living in again. I should have taken a semester off, but I felt that was not a good idea. I had to make myself get back into the mainstream of life.

In the early 1990s, I experienced a strange episode. I was sitting in a class at the University of Michigan. My classmates began to notice there was something wrong with me, but I told them I was fine. I was not fine; I was very dizzy. I quietly left the building and drove myself to the ER. I really needed a police officer that day and there wasn't one to be found.

I walked into St. Joseph Mercy Hospital and was quickly taken in. They discovered that the small hole at the top end of the shunt had a little clog. They treated the problem with IVs. The problem was gone within a few hours and I was fine again. I returned home that evening and I was back in school the next day.

There are many theories concerning the pressure inside my skull. One theory is that as a child my skull was growing, therefore the pressure did not build. In adult years the skull was fully developed allowing the pressure to build. I never had a headache as a child or in my early teens. I had fallen in the fourth grade and hit my head and had a slight concussion in 1968. I was treated and released by the University of Michigan Hospital and showed no signs of a problem. That fall could have caused the problem. That is just a theory, and not based on any medical facts.

Dr. Arno H. Fried of Hackensack University Medical Center in Hackensack, New Jersey, has some interesting findings regarding hydrocephalus:

> Teenagers and young adults can present for the first time with aqueductal stenosis and hydrocephalus.

This older group of patients usually presents with chronic headaches in the setting of having a head which is large on the growth chart, and there may be history of school problems and learning disabilities throughout the learning years of childhood. Appropriate imaging studies diagnose the problem, and if symptomatic, a VP shunt is recommended.[35]

Platybasia is a deformity where the angle formed by the basispheniod and the clivus, normally 130–140 degrees, is increased with flattening of the skull base. There is associated shortening of the basi-occipital bone and several malformations around the foramen magnum and cervical spine, such as Klippel-syndrome. The shortening of the skull base can lead to compression as the foramen magnum and cervical spine. Deformity of the skull base in achondroplasia contributes to the development of hydrocephalus in these children.[36]

I did not have a larger than normal head as a child. I did have a learning disability that is covered in Chapter 8. I do have the Klippel-syndrome. It has something to do with the shape and shortness of the back of the neck and some fusion of the vertebrae in the spine. I have 2 disks in my neck that are fused together. It has never been a problem to me.

I found it very interesting as to how shunting procedures began:

The modern shunting era began with Nulson and Spitz, creating a one-way pressure-regulated valve, which they placed in the atrium via the jugular vein. John Holter was the father of a hydrocephalic child who worked on the early development of the shunt valve. Becker and Nulson's landmark paper on the use of one-way ventricular atrial shunts set a new standard in hydrocephalus treatment, due to improved biomaterials such as silicone, and led the way for ventricular peritoneal shunts as today's standard.[37]

The word *hydrocephalus* comes to us from the Greek word the following quote explains:

Hydrocephalus, which, in Greek, translates as water (hydro) (cephalus), is an abnormal accumulation of cerebrospinal fluid within the ventricles (cavities) in the brain. CSF is produced in ventricles, circulates through the ventricular system and is then absorbed into the bloodstream. CSF protects the brain and the cord, contains nutrients and proteins that nourish the brain, and carries away waste. Hydrocephalus occurs when there is an imbalance between the amount of CSF that is produced and the rate at which it is absorbed.[38]

The advances made in the area of neurosurgery have helped millions around the world. As there are more studies in neurology, advanced research in neurosurgery will develop more cures for brain disabilities.

Chapter 8
Dyslexia

The most important area in education and development are learning the three Rs: reading, writing and arithmetic. They are vital for the success in learning the basics.

Dyslexia is a cruel disability in that it sets a person up for failure. Having said that, let me explain. My intelligence was not affected.

I learned from becoming a good listener. I loved to have someone read to me. As a child, I never missed out on the popular books that children read or were required to read. My mother read them to me. On one cold winter night my mother read *Old Yeller* from cover to cover without a break. She would finally tell me that she could not read anymore. I would tell her to get a drink of water so she could finish the book.

I was never able to accomplish learning math. I had a block that I could not break through and I slowly reached a point where I did not care.

I learned how to write checks and take care of my

checkbook, but I do have help to balance my checkbook. I worked for hours with special education teachers trying to learn long division. It has taken years, and I still have problems concerning math, spelling and writing. I will say, out of all of my setbacks in life, dyslexia was the only one that would bring me to tears. It is a hell of its own.

Many people in our society do not fully understand the problem with a learning disability nor do they understand the emotions that come with this problem.

Think about it like this. You have a lot of dreams and you start out to achieve them, and then you have a brick wall that stops you. I always wanted to be an engineer, and because of my math problem I could not achieve that. I am not sure where life would have led me if I had not had this learning disability.

I began school as a happy, bright child eager to learn. During elementary school it was discovered that I had a learning problem. I was not diagnosed with dyslexia at that time. Both my teachers and parents knew I had a problem. I was encouraged to work hard at my studies by my parents and teachers who were understanding and helpful.

I have listened to many theories concerning dyslexia. I have often heard that it means you read backwards, or see words backwards, for example: "saw" looks like "was." It is more than that. I can look at an entire sentence and flip-flop it so that the end phrase was not at the end but in the middle or even at the beginning. This was really hard for me to copy from the board or even just writing.

Everyday things concerning reading, writing, and math are different for me. To write anything, including this book, hours upon hours of editing have to be done. Even though I have a computer and a Franklin speller, I will still make mistakes. Whenever I write, I must have the material reviewed for mistakes. The computer has made it much easier to make the corrections.

During the 1960s and 1970s advancements in teaching and learning about learning disabilities were just beginning. Dyslexia is very complex, and is very different in each person.

In time I learned new ways to compensate for my disability, but I still have dyslexia. By avoiding the areas that I have difficulties in, I can almost make the problem seem to disappear. I require a structured environment without confusion. This is vital for my development and happiness.

One major problem I have is organizational skills. Many people with dyslexia have this problem. It is not necessary that the harder skills hold back a dyslexic person. Sometimes the simplest skills or tasks, such as easy math, simple spelling, and writing a note of easy words, are the hardest.

Most of my difficulties are in learning elementary math skills. On the other hand I am advanced in harder areas of study.

I still have memories of my mother and her pink curlers trying to teach me how to count. I hated those pink curlers. She would work with me, and I would become very stressed and I would not be allowed to leave the sofa until I had finished my work.

When educators came up with modern math, my mother would give me the problem and tell me to put the answer in the parenthesis; for example 8-( ) = 6. The answer was 2. I was totally confused.

My mother took a class in modern math to assist me. I know it was hard for her to find the time, and I do appreciate her working with me. Other problems were ( ) + 7 = 10. Now I know it was 3. But I have never figured out why they just didn't say 7+3 = 10. When you had long numbers like 14 + (4) – 2 = 16. I would just sit there and look at the page and wonder why I had to do this. Counting money was worse, but I did finally learn how. I use the Presidents' picture on each bill to tell how much the bill is worth.

I have always had problems counting money, and I depend on the honesty of others. I learned that most people are honest; however, I do make sure all my money is counted. I do not sign anything until it has been read to me and I fully understand what it says. I always have to review a document to make sure I don't make a mistake. This is when my ability to comprehend reading upsets me. I am always re-reading items, and I have a very hard time reading anything in cursive writing. I prefer type-written letters. If information is typed I have less problems. I do read books, but I am a very slow reader. I make myself read to keep what skills I have developed. I do the same with writing skills.

In first grade it was noticed that I skipped lines as I read. I learned to use a marker to help prevent this. I still use a marker to read.

I attended Holmes School until third grade, and then I attended Roosevelt, a private school on the campus of Eastern Michigan University. This school worked with my learning problem. At Roosevelt, if I was doing well in social studies, I was able to advance. If I was doing poorly in reading, math, or spelling skills, I would remain in the lower levels to work on those skills.

Roosevelt was a K–12 school. I was allowed to change classes in elementary and was given a hall locker. By changing classes, I would be with different grade levels. This allowed me to reach a higher intellectual level. The classes were staffed with student teachers from Eastern Michigan University. They would work with each student one on one, helping to improve their skills. I remember the reading lab being very hard, and I worked at spelling and writing along with math. During another hour I would be in a class of advanced social studies or art. In social studies, art and science I did very well.

In 1969, Roosevelt was closed, and I returned to Holmes Elementary. It was another year of hard work in my three Rs. I completed my sixth grade year and entered into junior high school in 1970. There my learning problem became an issue. Twice a week after school, Washtenaw Intermediate School District provided a special education tutor for me.

I was tutored from seventh grade until I graduated from high school. We mostly worked on writing and math. I was now doing well, but I was working very hard.

I remained "mainstreamed," which allowed me to excel in the areas that I could until I graduated from high school.

At Ypsilanti High School, I worked very hard in math. My math teacher also worked with me on my algebra and geometry. I feel that my math teacher really understood my learning problem.

During the 1960s, methods of teaching math and reading were changed. The teaching of phonics was stopped. I needed more focus on phonics. Later it was learned that I did not understand beginning sounds likes like "ph" or the ending of a word such as the "ing." I was not hearing impaired; I heard the sounds, but my brain did not process them. This was part of my learning problem. This would show in the way I pronounced a word, leaving out endings, and it shows in my spelling. I have worked very hard to improve my pronunciation. I was tested at Eastern Michigan University and Speech and Hearing at the University of Michigan.

It is now thought that the brain of a dyslexic looks different than the brain of a non-dyslexic. In the next few years, I believe that MRIs will become very helpful in the diagnosing of dyslexia.

The *Dictionary of Medical Terms* defines *dyslexic* as the following:

> Impairment of ability to read in which letters and words are reversed. Dyslexia, which affects more boys than girls, is usually linked to a central nervous system disorder, although some experts believe that it represents a complex of problems, possibly including visual defects, impaired hearing, stress, and inadequate instruction.[39]

To fully understand a dyslexic person, you, as a reader, would have to live with a dyslexic or be dyslexic yourself. There are times I have such frustration in trying to do the simplest task that it will overwhelm me. Age is allowing me to overcome some of this frustration.

I felt that college was a war, so to speak, and I decided I was going to win it. One thing I had going for me was that getting a low grade didn't bother me. That was just part of going to school.

I cannot tell how many times in my life that I wished I did not have dyslexia. I often wished I could read, write and do math without difficulty. I sometimes feel like I invented run-on sentences and fragments.

I loved to visit the writing labs while I was in college, and I worked to learn as much as I could about writing and grammar. I feel that people with the ability to read, write and do math have a gift, and they should never waste it.

I would love to work with medical researchers on dyslexia who are working to discover a medication or a surgical method to free people of this hidden disability.

I am an oral learner, and when given instructions orally I remember them and understand them. I never have problems giving lectures because I am following my own notes.

When I was a student at the University of Alabama, a writing instructor sent me to the writing lab. There I worked very hard on my skills. All of my exams were written and it was hard for me. One instructor for world literature figured out my problem, and he helped me take my exam. I answered a few questions that he knew I knew the answer to. He knew I was dyslexic.

After I returned to Eastern Michigan University, I was sent to the reading lab, and a friend worked with me. I then was tested and it was found I was dyslexic, and I then was re-tested in the Speech and Hearing Department at the University of Michigan, and they had the same findings as Eastern Michigan University. I had a severe learning problem, and at last I was given oral exams while getting my degree in history.

I did not use the Library for the Blind for my textbooks. I had to read my books. At times I became so frustrated that I asked my mother to read the books to me

When I began attending the School of Natural Resources and Environment, I went to the Disabled Students Department. There I gave them a letter about my learning problems, and we worked out a special program to assist with my dyslexia. I was provided with a note taker. This was a specific student in the same class who provided me with a copy of their notes. I also had to take notes in class since the professors were watching to see if I could keep up. I had all my books recorded at the Library for the Blind and all of my exams were oral. I had a tape recorder that I bought to record lectures.

I never had any problems, and my instructors worked with me and encouraged me in my studies. I also worked very hard.

I would buy two textbooks, and they would be sent to the Library of the Blind in Princeton, New Jersey. The books would be recorded and one book returned to me. The books had to be sent 2 months prior to the beginning of the semester. They were always very prompt in getting the books recorded and returned before the beginning of my classes. I would then read along with the tape of the required chapters.

When I was given handouts or articles in class, I would sometimes use the special library for the disabled on campus. I would use the Kurzweil Machine for reading.

I would record all lectures I attended as well as take notes. When class was over, I would copy the notes that the note taker provided. I would then study and listen to the tapes and review all of my notes. Then I would get ready for the oral exam. I was able to maintain a B average at the University of Michigan.

Finally when I was a student at the University of Michigan, the Vocational Rehabilitation Department provided funds to pay for my writing tutor.

I would begin my papers the first week of the semester to be sure all deadlines were met. I worked with a writing tutor to insure that the papers were correct. Then I got them edited and typed. I always had to pay the tutor and typist. That was another part of going to college, which added to my cost of college. I learned my way around the library. I did not like the card catalog, and instead I learned where the history or science books were kept. I then memorized the area and was able to locate the book I needed. I would only run into problems when the stacks were changed.

Today the computer catalogue is very easy for me to use. I still work to learn the lay out of the library and location of the stacks. There were times people thought I was studying in the library when I was just learning the subject areas and the layout of the building. I could not read or understand the maps on the wall.

I have problems reading road maps, but after I get to a place, I can remember how to return. I go by landmarks, which can be a problem if I have to make a detour.

Whenever I move to a new area, I take a day and drive all the different routes. Then I have learned where things are located. I am unable to give good directions, but I can send you in the right direction. Where you will arrive is another question.

I learned that color coding is a very good tool for me. Many different things are used to work with learning disabilities. For one example, many people use the colored glasses. They never worked for me.

Dyslexia is neurological and can be inherited. More research is being done concerning the brain, and more is being learned about dyslexia. Dyslexia is a hidden disability. Most dyslexics like myself are hard workers and work to achieve goals. Every person is different with or without dyslexia, and all people learn in different ways.

The following tests are some of the ones that I was given in college to better understand my dyslexia. I just remember that each test lasted for 4 hours.

Halstead-Reitan Neuropsychological Test Battery.
Wechsler Memory Scale—Revised (WMS)
Developmental Test of Visual-Motor Integration (VMI)
Rey-Osterreith Figure
Wide-Range Achievement Test—Revised (WRAT-R)
Peabody Picture Vocabulary Test—Revised (PPVT-R)
Metropolitan Reading Test
Bender-Gestalt Test
Millon Clinical Multiaxial Inventory

After my testing was done, the psychologist explained that I needed oral testing for my exams in college and that I needed to use a tape recorder for lectures.

My tests revealed that I was reading at a fifth grade level and that my math was below fifth grade level. My writing was worse. One psychologist told me that, according to the test results, I should not have been able to obtain a college degree. But I did not only receive one degree; I received 2 bachelor's degrees. One was in history and one was in fish biology.

I hope that psychologists are researching to develop new forms of testing for dyslexia.

I finished my degree in history at Eastern Michigan University in 1982. In 1988, I began a degree in Fish Biology at the University of Michigan in Ann Arbor. I completed that degree in 1992.

I am hoping that community colleges develop more hands-on programs. This would be an excellent area for LD people to receive training for employment. I do feel that the advances in technology will be one of the best aids to people with dyslexia.

Chapter 9
Employment/Lawsuit

I was taught to work, and I never wanted to be any kind of a burden on society. I feel that all Americans have a right to work and should try, if at all possible and if their health allows them to work. I knew that my skills were limited due to my dyslexia and physical disabilities. This was made very clear when I began to look for work. During my time of job hunting, I would sometimes work minimum wage jobs to hold me over financially. Sometimes I worked three jobs at a time to support myself.

Most people don't have the faintest idea of how hard it is for a disabled person to locate a job. With a bad hip and dyslexia, looking for work was very hard. If the job required lots of standing and walking I was limited and also my typing ability was limited.

The one issue that is never addressed is that many disabled people face a very low pay scale after being hired in most cases. There are the exceptions, and this will depend completely on the disability. If I had only had dyslexia, I would have joined the armed services after I finished college.

Finding employment as a disabled person is a real trip! It's not what any able-bodied person understands. There are people who think the disabled can easily get any job they want. This is not true, and only disabled people, their families, and their doctors know this.

The Rehabilitation Act of 1973 is to protect disabled people. It was followed by the Americans with Disabilities Act (ADA Act), which also protects disabled people. But a disabled person must understand that the Rehabilitation Act and ADA Act cannot promise a job or always give protection to a disabled person in the job market. A disabled person could fall under the Civil Rights Act of 1964, because everyone has a right to work if at all possible.

There are many disabled people who are facing discrimination in private as well as government sectors. The main problem is that most disabled people will not speak out to defend themselves. They just accept what happens to them. I worried about being able to live comfortably and provide for myself.

I know that social services and churches can be helpful, but the bottom line is money. I was forced to live on a very small income even though at the time I was working three jobs and I had a bachelor's degree and was studying for my second degree.

Even after working hard, a person could have their Social Security payments lower than expected because they worked at lower paying jobs

Employment is a form of red tape for a disabled person. My disability became an issue in my life when I began looking for employment after I received my first degree. I searched for jobs and received over 300 rejections in the early 1980s. Some were from private employers and some were from U.S. government agencies.

I would like to try and explain to the reader the steps I had to take to obtain employment with the United States government. I had to complete the following steps, as does every disabled person who seeks employment with the federal government.

First, I had to use the State Vocational Rehabilitation Services and work with a state rehab counselor.

Second, I had to complete a 171 application. This is a standard U.S. government application that is 4 pages long. The 171 application should be typed. I always had to pay someone to type this for me. I finally realized that I could have copies made and not keep paying a typist. The application was then sent to agencies along with a letter from the rehabilitation counselor and with doctors' letters concerning my disability.

I was told that the application could be filled out in black ink; try that with dyslexia!

After completing the application and finding a position, I then had to complete a 700-hour job appointment. This is about three months of working at a job that is not permanent. After the 700 hours I found that there was no permanent position to move into. I had to start looking all over again!

Third, after about a year I was hired through the Schedule A appointment. The Schedule A was created for the placement of people with disabilities. There is a two-year-long probation period with this type of appointment. I could be hired through Schedule A only after completing a 700-hour appointment. I also had to complete another 171 application.

When a person is hired under the Schedule A appointment, that person is not put on the job register. They will not be in the pool of potential employees to be considered. The job seeker has to contact each department that has a job opening they could perform.

If a government agency was interested in me, I had to contact my rehabilitation counselor so that she could visit the site. This was to see if there were any special equipment I needed or if the employer had any questions.

Vocational rehabilitation helps to meet the needs of the disabled. They can and will protect the rights of the disabled person.

I was hired on June 6, 1983, and completed the 700-hour appointment at Milan Federal Prison in Milan, Michigan. I began my career as a file clerk at the Milan Federal Prison. There was no typing in this position. I was unable to type at any speed except slow. I was able to perform my file clerk's job. In September at the end of the appointment, I found out that there was no permanent position for me there.

It took me until December 3, 1984 to locate another job. I was hired as a file clerk in the personnel office at the Bureau of Prisons in Springfield, Missouri. That job was through the Schedule A appointment. I followed all the requirements and guidelines for the hiring of the disabled for the federal government.

Now I was to begin my two-year Schedule A appointment probation period. This is given to allow the disabled person a chance to compete.

The Department of Justice has many good, hard-working employees within its large agency. The actions taken by a few employees at the federal prison in Springfield, Missouri, is not a reflection on the Department of Justice as a whole or the Springfield Federal Prison.

The personnel officer (I'll refer to him as Officer A), who hired me as a file clerk and with whom I worked well with transferred to Washington, DC. I had received good job evaluations from Officer A. After I arrived, I was placed in a temporary position as a clerk typist even though I was a permanent employee.

With the arrival of the new personnel officer (I'll refer to him as Officer X), my problems soon began. He would talk about how he went to church and how happy he was to be back at Springfield. I would listen to him and watch him.

On a bright sunny morning, Officer X called me into his office. He told me that I was in a temporary position and he was going to fire me. He suggested that I should resign. Officer X felt that my performance was poor. He wanted me to file a complaint against Officer A, who hired me. I figured out this was probably because Officer A had lost an earlier EEOC case. I did not say a word and left the impression I was going to do what Officer X wanted. But that is when I called the FBI and met with the federal attorney.

This was a hard decision to make, and one that I wished never had to be made. I was a permanent employee with excellent references, including an FBI agent who knew me from a prior job search. I contacted the FBI at the first sign of discrimination. Then I had a meeting with the federal attorney. The federal attorney contacted the FBI in Springfield.

I would soon learn that a medical doctor had filed and won an earlier discrimination case against Officer A. I wasn't the first disabled employee to have a problem at this federal prison.

I called Personnel Officer A in Washington DC and explained what was going on. I could not get a transfer because Personnel Officer X was stating that I was not a permanent employee.

Personnel Officer X was breaking the law, and he did not seem to know that I was a permanent employee. He should have known that; I think he thought I was an idiot. I also contacted my caseworker in Michigan, who at that time told me to remain there and see if Officer X would fire me. I was told what steps to take and how to follow through. Officer X never did fire me.

I also contacted the union representative. I was not a union member, but they helped me. The union representative and I had a meeting with Personnel Officer X. During that meeting he admitted to the union representative that he was going to fire me. The union representative was taking notes during these meetings. I then copied my personnel file while Officer X watched.

It was in August of 1985 that I finally resigned under protest. My nerves could not take this situation. Also during this time, my father was fighting cancer.

The day I left, I wrote out my reasons for resigning. This was a problem for Personnel Officer X. He did not like what I had written and wanted it changed. He told me it was going to hurt me later in looking for work. It did not have that effect.

After I returned to Ann Arbor, Michigan, and I visited with an FBI agent. Later a friend referred me to Attorney Jean L. King. She took the proper steps to file a discrimination case on my behalf against the Springfield Medical Center for Federal Prisoners in Springfield, Missouri, in late 1984. At the time this case was heard, I was no longer an employee of the Department of Justice.

My lawyer was able to contact the medical doctor's lawyer from the first case after the investigation began. This was very helpful in my case. I went to work for Jean L. King and the Department of the Interior while I was attending the University of Michigan and awaiting the outcome of the case. I also worked for Pinckney Recreation Area as a park ranger. I enjoyed working at the park and being outside. I got along well with all of my supervisors and other coworkers at the Recreation area.

I also worked at Greenfield Village in Dearborn, Michigan, giving historical lectures within the village. This was an interesting job.

I feel there were times during the investigation of this case that it could have been resolved without going to court. Finally a hearing was held on December 13, 1989, in Springfield, Missouri. A federal attorney did not represent Personal Officer X. He was represented by someone from the Bureau of Prisons. I expected to see a federal attorney and one was not present.

I collected evidence during that last month at work. For example: Officer X left notes on my desk that made no sense, and I kept notes. This information would be used in the federal hearing. My caseworker at Michigan Vocational Rehabilitation was informed of the hearing. The union representative wrote an affidavit from information heard in the meetings with Personnel Officer X. This affidavit, along with others, was used in court in my defense.

Before the hearing began, Personnel Officer X contacted a young woman from Kelly Services to record the hearing and type up the information. During the hearing, the federal judge noticed the woman in the back of the courtroom with a boom box. She asked the woman to come forward and questioned her about her business in the courtroom. The judge was furious and had the woman removed. She had a federal court recorder called in. The judge then called in Officer X, and she was very upset that they had not made arrangements for a federal court recorder.

After all that, the judge told Mrs. King that she could call her first witness. We then learned that Personnel Officer X had sent the witness home. He told the judge that it was getting late. The judge was very upset again with Officer X. The hearing was held up about 30 minutes to an hour. The witness had to give her testimony over a speakerphone.

When the hearing began, it was interesting listening to the testimony. No one really knew what was going on, and it was very evident that the handicap specialist did not have training in the area of handicap placement. That came out with cross-examination.

It was learned during testimony that neither Michigan Rehabilitation nor Missouri Rehabilitation received a call from Officer X concerning any problems with my job performance. He would have received help if he had called. This would have been part of the handicap specialist or Personnel Officers X's job.

Personnel Officer X was cross-examined by my attorney and the federal judge. The facts were easily found. It was a case of being placed into a temporary position with permanent status.

Personnel Officer A testified before the federal judge that my position was permanent, but he made the mistake of not changing my status from temporary clerk typist to permanent file clerk. If he had done this, the entire episode might have been avoided. He explained that he was told that I only typed 12 words per minute by me over the phone.

I won the case. I was told that Personnel Officer X was placed on probation because of his discrimination against me. I do not know if this is true. I do know that I have never received a letter of apology from him.

During the years that I was waiting for my case to be heard, I worked at minimum wage jobs to support myself. As the case was settled, I had to report all of those years from those low wages. The earnings from those jobs were deducted from my settlement. Looking back I should have just stayed home out of the freezing Michigan cold. I would have gotten all of my back pay, and my leg and hip pain might not have forced me to retire as early as it did.

I soon learned that Jean L. King was an excellent attorney, and we became friends. I feel that my case was won because I was honest and followed the correct steps for the hiring of the handicapped within the United States government.

The case was appealed by the Bureau of Prisons, but the decision was not overturned. Even though this occurred over 20 years ago, I will always remember the events and the people involved.

This event cost me time from my employment and advancement within the government agency. I only asked for my back pay and to reinstate my time of employment. When the dust settled, this added up to 10 years of service.

After the case was settled, I worked in the Department of Interior until I began to have problems with my hip and legs. Due to the dyslexia and the hip, plus the fear that the lab was going to be closed in Ann Arbor, I decided to take a medical retirement. During this time, other people retired from this lab because of its possible closure. I knew that if the lab closed it was going to be very difficult for me to locate another job with all my problems. I did not want to gamble with that possibility. I don't think anyone would.

Attorney Mrs. Jean L. King

Chapter 10
Life Today

Today my home is located in Tennessee. Life is much slower and very peaceful. I spend time painting and listening to history books as well as reading history. I go to historical lectures held at Vanderbilt and in the surrounding area. I have become active within different groups.

I still work at writing to keep my skills up and my mind active. I know, because of my dyslexia, it is very important that I work at my three Rs. I have done history lectures on Native Americans. I enjoy doing painting and find that to be relaxing.

I must say I have thought about my years of employment, the good and the bad. I know that these years were very stressful. Time has taken away the stress but not the memory. I often wonder why this all happened? If I say I wasn't bitter during some of my employment then I am not being totally honest.

I hope there is not a disabled person going through what I had to go through. I feel that times have changed in regards to the placement of the disabled, but there still are problems that the disabled face in the work force. This is an issue that will never go away.

I often enjoy sitting in the late afternoon watching the sun gently drift out of sight in the western sky. The cool air blows across the fields as darkness creeps over the landscape. The crickets sing and the lighting bugs dance about the yard; that is when I think about my life

My life is one I have enjoyed. I have had many problems to overcome, but everyone does. I have lived a life without perfection through the good and the bad times. I have learned about the real world. It can be kind and it can be cruel. I am glad I live in a free nation where I can stand up for my rights. I would never have made it through life without my family, my friends and my faith in God.

Chapter Notes

Chapter 1

[1] J. M. Lackie and J.A.T. Dow, *The Dictionary of Cell & Molecular Biology,* 3rd ed. (London: Academic Press, 1999) <http://www.mblad.gla.ac.uk/~julian/news.html>.

[2] Victor L. Yu, MD, "Serratia Marcescens: Historical Perspective and Clinical Review," *New England Journal of Medicine* 300 (April 19, 1979): 887-863.

[3] Yu, 887.

[4] Yu, 887.

[5] Yu, 888.

[6] Yu, 889.

[7] J. W. Scharf, F. Wild and J. P. Guggenbichler, "Monatsschr Kinderheilkd," *Springer-Verlag 1991,* 139, 10 (Oct. 1991):695-8. (Infection with Serratia marcescens in newborn infants—clinical aspects, therapy and disease course).

[8] U.S. Army, *U. S. Army Activity in the U.S. Biological Warfare Programs* 1 and 2 (February 24, 1977): 22-59, 60-234. (Unclassified.) <http://www.gwu.edu/%7Ensarchiv/NSAEBB/NSAEBB58/RNCBW_USABWP.pdf>.

[9] U.S. Army, 33.

[10] U.S. Army, 41-42.

[11] U.S. Army, 87-91,

[12] U.S. Army, 172-173.

[13] Philippe Berthelot, MD, MPH; Florence Grattard, MD, PhD; Collette Amerger, RN; Marie-Claude Frery, DrPH; Frederic Lucht, MD; Bruno Pozzetto, MD, PhD; Phillippe Fragier, MD, "Investigation of Nosocomial Outbreak Due to Serratia Marcescens in a Maternity Hospital," *ICHE* 20, 4

(April 1999): 233 <http://www.slackinc.com/general/iche/stor0499/4ber.htm>.

Chapter 3

[14] Paul Schnur, MD, Pamela Hait, John Everson, webmaster, "The History of Plastic Surgery, ASPS and PSEF": 1-7 <http://www.plasticsurgery.org/overview/pshistory.html>.

[15] Schnur, 1-7.

[16] Schnur, 1-7.

[17] Schnur, 1-7.

[18] "Obituary of Dr. Harold Delfe Gillies," *The Lancet 1960,* September 17, 1960: 655-656.

[19] "History Coming of Age...The History of the AAFPRS," (American Academy of Facial Plastic Surgery and Reconstructive Surgery) <http://www.facial-plastic-surgery.org/patient/about_us/h_war.html>: 1-2.

[20] "History Coming of Age...The History of The AAFPRS," 1-3.

[21] "History Coming of Age...The History of The AAFPRS," 1-2.

[22] "History of Plastic Surgery at the University of Michigan," (University of Michigan Department of Plastic Surgery) <http://www.surgery.med.umich.edu/plastic/sectional_history/history.htm>: 1-3.

Chapter 5

[23] John B. Roberts, AM, MD, FACS, *War Surgery of the Face* (New York, New York: William Wood and Company, 1919), 4.

[24] B. Travers, ed., source: "Dental History Orthodontics," *World of Invention,* (Gale, 1994), 457. <http://www.gumshield.com/history/orthodontics.html> (2002-2003): 1-2.

[25] "Dental History of Orthodontics," 1-2.

[26] "Dental History of Orthodontics," 1-2.

Chapter 7

[27] Audry Nicolas, *L'Orthopedie Introduction: Volume 1* (Royal College and Senior Dean of the Faculty of Physick at Paris, 1658-1742).

[28] Peter Nakaji, MD, "What is Neurosurgery?" <http://neurosurgery.ucsd.edu/history.html> (March 17, 2003): 1-3.

[29] Nakaji, 1-3.

[30] Nakaji, 1-3.

[31] Lawrence McHenry, Jr., CBA, MD, *History of Neurology* (Springfield, Illinois: Charles C. Thomas Publishers, Ltd, 1969) 3,7.

[32] McHenry, Jr., 8,10.

[33] McHenry, Jr., 8,10.

[34] Arno H. Fried, MD, "Childhood Hydrocephalus: Clinical Features, Treatment, and the Slit-Ventricle Syndrome," <www.gliadel.comhttp://virtualtrials.com/shuntsefm> (March 17, 2003): 5-33.

[35] Fried, 6-33.

[36] Fried, 3-33.

[37] "Treatments /Programs," Cedars-Sinai Health System, <http://www.cedars-sinai.edu/mdnsi/3584.asp> (March 17, 2003): 1-3.

[38]

Chapter 8

[39] Mikel A. Rothenberg, MD and Charles F. Chapman, *Dictionary of Medical Terms,* 3rd ed.: 1989,1984.